UNDERSTANDING *the* PERSONALITY *of the* HOLY SPIRIT

UNDERSTANDING *the* PERSONALITY *of the* HOLY SPIRIT

· BOOK **I** ·

FUCHSIA PICKETT

Charisma®
HOUSE
A STRANG COMPANY

Most STRANG COMMUNICATIONS/CHARISMA HOUSE/SILOAM products are available at special quantity discounts for bulk purchase for sales promotions, premiums, fund-raising, and educational needs. For details, write Strang Communications/Charisma House/Siloam, 600 Rinehart Road, Lake Mary, Florida 32746, or telephone (407) 333-0600.

UNDERSTANDING THE PERSONALITY OF THE HOLY SPIRIT by Fuchsia Pickett
Published by Charisma House
A Strang Company
600 Rinehart Road
Lake Mary, Florida 32746
www.charismahouse.com

Unless otherwise noted, all Scripture quotations are from the King James Version of the Bible.

Scripture quotations marked ASV are from the American Standard Bible. Copyright © 1901. Public domain.

Scripture quotations marked NAS are from the New American Standard Bible. Copyright © 1960, 1962, 1963, 1968, 1971, 1972, 1973, 1975, 1977, by the Lockman Foundation. Used by permission. (www.Lockman.org).

Scripture quotations marked NIV are from the Holy Bible, New International version. Copyright © 1973, 1978, 1984, International Bible Society. Used by permission.

Scripture quotations marked PHILLIPS are from *The New Testament in Modern English*, Revised Edition. Copyright © 1958, 1960, 1972 by J. B. Phillips. Macmillan Publishing Co. Used by permission.

Cover design by Rachel Campbell

Library of Congress Cataloging-in-Publication Data:
Pickett, Fuchsia T.
 Understanding the personality of the Holy Spirit/Fuchsia Pickett.
    p. cm.
 ISBN 1-59185-283-8
 1. Holy Spirit. I. Title.
 BT121.3.P53 2004
 231'.3--dc22

                                    2003021563

04 05 06 07   8 7 6 5 4 3 2 1
Printed in the United States of America

Contents

Introduction

Some readers might think it rather abstract and impractical to write a book that answers the question, "Who is the Holy Spirit?" Others may deem it presumptuous of me to say, "I would like to present to you the Holy Spirit." To many people the Holy Spirit is nothing more than a name in a religious creed recited in liturgical services. To others He is merely a vague influence mentioned in the Scriptures. Even those Christians who think they know who the Holy Spirit is many times do not recognize Him as a divine Person. I do not blame anyone for thinking about the Holy Spirit in these ways, for I remember the time in my life when I too would have thought it strange to address the Holy Spirit as a personal Friend and Teacher. Even though I referred to Him as the

Third Person of the Godhead, when speaking theologically, He was not a real Person to me.

The doctrine of the Holy Spirit as a divine Personality is not only extremely practical, but also fundamental to our knowledge of God and our relationship to Him. Anyone who knows God the Father and God the Son without having a true understanding of God the Holy Spirit has not attained the Christian conception of God, nor has he come to the fullness of Christian experience.

I must mention the doctrine of the Trinity here to give us a proper foundation for the study of the Holy Spirit. In Genesis 1:26 reference is made to the plurality that exists in the Godhead: "And God said, Let us make man in our image, after our likeness." God referred to "our" image and "our" likeness, using plural pronouns to refer to Himself. Many such references confirm the reality of the Triune Godhead. Even the passage in Deuteronomy that some use to discount the validity of the Trinity actually confirms the fact of the Trinity. We read there, "Jehovah our God is one Jehovah" (Deut. 6:4, ASV). The Hebrew word for God that is used here is a plural form. That indicates, in spite of the intense monotheism of the Hebrews, the plurality of persons in the one Godhead. So we refer to the Godhead in its original state, in the eons of eternity, as the Triune Godhead. Our study here focuses on the Person of the Holy Spirit, but we cannot ignore His integral relationship to the Triune Godhead.

The importance of understanding the Person of the Holy Spirit is seen first of all in His effect on our perspective of worship. If we think of the Holy Spirit as merely an impersonal influence or divine power, we will inevitably rob Him of the honor and the worship He is due. We will not relate to Him properly or give Him the love, trust, surrender, and obedience that we should. We need to acknowledge this Third Person of the Godhead as He does His work on the earth, and yield to Him in complete obedience to His will.

It is important that we not relate to the Holy Spirit only as an influence or power so we don't try to "use" Him, or "it," for our own purposes. This mistaken concept of the Holy Spirit inevitably leads to self-exaltation. It causes us to strut in pride, thinking that we have received the Holy Spirit and therefore belong to a superior order of Christians. Instead we need to think of Him correctly in the biblical way—as a divine Person of defined majesty and glory. Then we will relate to Him properly by asking questions such as: "How can I surrender more completely to the Holy Spirit?" "How can the Holy Spirit possess me and use me in a greater way?" Relating to the Holy Spirit as a divine Person is one of the most fundamental truths of the Bible—one that we must understand if we are to enjoy right relationship with God. Many earnest Christians are going astray on this point. They are trying to obtain some divine power they can use according to their will or giftings instead of surrendering their lives to the Person of the Holy Spirit. True maturity in Christ only comes through cultivating a right relationship with the Holy Spirit.

We need to acknowledge the Holy Spirit as a divine Person of infinite majesty who has come to dwell in our hearts, take possession of us, and work out God's eternal plan and predestined will in us, for us, and through us, until we are a praise to the glory of the Father. Then we will experience true holiness in the reality of self-renunciation, self-abnegation, and self-humiliation. I know of no other truth that can humble us and put us on our faces before God more quickly than this: The blessed Holy Spirit is the Third Person of the Godhead who has come to dwell in our hearts and to restore us to the image of our God as He, in His infinite wisdom, unfolds His predestined plan for our lives. Such love and infinite desire of the Godhead to dwell with mankind is incomprehensible to our finite minds.

Many Christians testify to the entire transformation of their lives and service to God when they become acquainted with the Holy Spirit as a Person. That is my personal testimony as well. After serving God as a Methodist professor and pastor for many years, I came into a fuller relationship with the Holy Spirit. I realized then that Someone had come to live in my life, Someone with whom I was not personally or intimately acquainted. When I surrendered my life completely to Him, He began to reveal to me that He had come to be my Teacher. He had come to unveil the Christ who had been living in me for seventeen years. It was then that I began to become intimately acquainted with the Holy Spirit as a Person.

People often misunderstand what we are saying when we refer to the Holy Spirit as a Person. They think we are saying that He has hands, eyes, and ears and operates in a physical body as we know it. But those physical characteristics are attributes of corporeality, not personality. The generally accepted attributes of personality are intellect, volition, and emotions—knowledge, will, and feelings. One who thinks, feels, and exercises his will is a person.

We finite human beings will one day lose our corporeality. Our earthly life in this world will end, and we will depart from these bodies. That does not mean we will cease to be persons, however. The Bible says that when we are absent from the body, we are present with the Lord (2 Cor. 5:23). So we will be alive in the presence of the Lord without mortal bodies.

The Scriptures ascribe to the Holy Spirit all the attributes of personality, which we have defined here, that make Him a divine Person. For example, knowledge is attributed to the Holy Spirit in the passage that says, "Even so the thoughts of God no one knows except the Spirit of God" (1 Cor. 2:11, NAS). The Holy Spirit is not just illumination or inspiration that comes to our minds so we can see truth. He is a Person who Himself knows the things of God and reveals them to us. We know also that the Holy Spirit came to instruct us, to become our Teacher. Jesus said, "But the Counselor, the Holy Spirit, whom the Father will send in my name, will teach you all things and will remind you of everything I have said to you" (John 14:26, NIV). It is our privilege today to have the Holy Spirit, a living Person, dwelling within us, opening the classroom of our spirits twenty-four hours a day and letting us ask about anything we want to know. He never closes the classroom, and He never scolds us for asking. It is wonderful to know that, as we study the Bible, we have the divine Author of the Book to interpret it and to teach us its real and innermost meaning according to His divine knowledge.

Volition, or will, is attributed to the Holy Spirit in the Scriptures that teach us concerning the gifts of the Spirit: "But all these worketh that one and the selfsame Spirit, dividing to each man severally as he will" (1 Cor. 12: 11). The Holy Spirit came to earth to fulfill the will of God in the earth. *Emotion* is also attributed to Him in Paul's appeal to the Romans for prayer: "Now I beseech you, brethren, for the Lord Jesus Christ's sake, and for the love of the Spirit, that ye strive together with me in your prayers to God for me" (Rom. 15:30). Notice particularly the phrase, "the love of the Spirit." Isn't that a wonderful thought? It demonstrates that the Holy Spirit is not a blind influence or an "it." He is not tongues or gifts or just divine power. He is a divine Person, the Third Person of the Godhead, living in us and loving us with the tenderest love.

Have you ever thanked the Holy Spirit for His love? We think of God the Father who "so loved the world, that he gave his only begotten Son" (John 3:16). We speak of Jesus' love for the Church being so great that He suffered outside the city wall in order to sanctify unto Himself a glorious Church. But have we considered "the love of the Spirit"? Often we thank our heavenly Father for His great love to us. We thank Jesus for loving us enough to die for us. Have we ever knelt in reverence to the Holy Spirit and thanked Him for His great love for us?

Yet we owe our salvation as truly to the love of the

Spirit as we do to the love of the Father and the Son. If the Holy Spirit had not become the willing Servant to come to the world and seek out our lost condition and bring conviction to us, we could not have come to the Savior. I think we have missed a lot by not realizing who this blessed Third Person of the Godhead is. We have not fully understood the love He has for us, and the hurt-love He still experiences as a servant bringing us back to the Father's house.

I think if I tried to briefly summarize the message of this book, I would shout to the Church today, "This blessed Holy Spirit, the Third Person of the Godhead, is not an *it!* He is not a fleshly manifestation of *religious* people jerking their bodies. He is not just tongues or gifts. He is much more than an *influence.* He is the infinite, omnipotent, omniscient, omnipresent, eternal Third Person of the Triune Godhead! He is a divine Person!"

I'm sure this is not a new concept to many. But I wonder how it affects our lives in a practical way. Do we treat the Holy Spirit as a Person? Do we honor Him, love Him, and acknowledge Him? Have we learned to communicate with Him? Do we know communion with the Holy Spirit, which the Bible teaches we can have? Do we think of Him as One who is alongside us, in us, helping us, comforting us? Have we experienced His divine comradeship? His companionship?

My whole purpose in writing this book is to present my Friend and Teacher as He has revealed Himself through the Scriptures to me personally. As we study the personality of this Third Person of the Godhead as the

Bible describes Him, it is my prayer that we come to know the blessed Holy Spirit in a more intimate and personal way and to learn to yield to Him and cooperate with Him more fully. It is with this desire that this book is presented to the body of Christ.

Relationship With a Divine Personality

M odern theologians have declared this age to be the age of the Holy Spirit. The Holy Spirit came to earth on the Day of Pentecost and has remained here to do the work the Father sent Him to do. He will not leave until God's eternal plan is accomplished. He came to fulfill the purpose God had for the Church, to fulfill what God had promised and prophesied in the Scriptures for hundreds of years. He was the Father's gift to the Church, sent under divine mandate to be the Chief Administrator of God's kingdom on earth.

Today's Church must come to a right relationship with the Holy Spirit in order for the kingdom of God to develop on earth as God has ordained. It is not enough for Christians to recite a liturgical creed that only mentions the Holy Spirit; neither is it enough to simply understand the doctrine of the Holy Spirit. The Holy Spirit is a divine Person sent to do a supernatural work in the lives of men and women who choose to know God. We need to become acquainted with the Holy Spirit as a Person to fulfill the purposes of God in our personal lives and in our churches. Only as we develop an intimate relationship with this Third Person of the Godhead can we hope to realize the abundant life that Jesus promised to all who followed Him.

It is unfortunate that even the evangelical church world often calls the Holy Spirit an "it" or describes Him as "tongues" or defines Him as an "emblem" like the dove or the wind. Some declare Him to be a mere "influence" or "power." He is none of those things! He is the Third Person of the Godhead who came to bring us into right relationship with God. The Holy Spirit wants us to commune and fellowship with Him in an intimacy that is greater than any we would share with another person. Many of us do not enjoy this kind of relationship with the Holy Spirit because we do not think of Him as a Person. We could even have received the baptism of the Holy Spirit and still not recognize Him as a divine Personality. Before we can relate to the Holy Spirit properly, we must accept the truth that He is, in fact, a Person.

What Constitutes Personality?

When using the word *personality*, we simply refer to "the quality or state of being a person." Being a person involves the power of *intellect*, or the mind; the power of *volition*, or the will; and the power of *emotional response*. In the populace of the world, these three aspects of personality combine to form such infinite variations of persons that we can truly say no two people on the face of the earth are alike.

There are many scientific approaches to understanding personality. Some have resulted in major branches of scientific study, such as psychology. For those who have researched it, the psyche has proved to be quite enigmatic in its complexities. The behavioral sciences have drawn their conclusions about man's "typical" behavior, only to find that they must constantly adjust those conclusions as man's behavior changes. Unfortunately, too many of these scientists have never come into a relationship with God, who created the human psyche. Therefore, they have unwittingly abandoned the only valid premise for true knowledge and understanding of man. Without a relationship with God, it is impossible for man to understand either God or himself. True comprehension of God and man results only from a relationship with God; after all, He defined the purpose of man in creation.

The three definitive elements of personality, then, include the *mind, will*, and *emotional response*. Only as we learn to recognize and properly relate to these three aspects of the personality of the Holy Spirit can we intimately fellowship with Him as a divine Person. As the Third Person of the Godhead, the Holy Spirit reveals the mind of God as He fulfills the will of God for mankind. He also expresses the emotions of God in His loving and holy relationship to mankind.

The Holy Spirit simply has come to reveal Jesus, the lovely Savior, to all who will respond to His invitation to receive eternal life. The Spirit offers eternal life to all who will accept the sacrifice of Jesus' blood for their sins. Only the Holy Spirit has the power to save our souls and change us into the image of Christ. But it is when we accept that sacrifice for our sins that we can begin to know what the Father intended for man when He created Him.

The Personality of Man

When God created man as a tripartite person with a body, a soul, and a spirit, He intended man to live in fellowship with Himself. God created man's body, perfectly adapted to Earth's environment, to be a home for man's soul and spirit. Man's soul, his personality, allowed him to respond to all of life in God's beautiful earth. Man's spirit allowed him to commune with God, who is Spirit.

God had warned Adam that in the day he ate of the fruit of the tree of the knowledge of good and evil, he would die (Gen. 2:16–17). But when the serpent deceived Adam's wife, he told her that they would not die if they ate of that tree. He declared that, instead, they themselves would become as gods (Gen. 3:4–5). Yet God's Word was true, and when Adam and his wife ate of the forbidden fruit, their spirits died to God. It severed their relationship with Him. Thus, all mankind was doomed to live eternally in that state of being ruled by their souls, with no possibility of communion with God.

In a terrible sense, mankind has fulfilled the serpent's

word to the first couple that they would be "as gods." Since the beginning of time nations have ravaged each other in an attempt to satisfy man's ungodly lust for power, for sovereignty, for dominion over other men. Without the life of God influencing man through his spirit, man's soul became warped and twisted. His mind turned hostile to God, his will became self-centered, and his emotions were filled with anger, envy, hatred, the desire to rule, and other negative forces. Man's personality was doomed to ultimate destruction.

Still, God had a plan to reverse that verdict, and He has been unfolding that plan since the beginning of time. God's eternal plan was to have a family with whom He could fellowship throughout all eternity. Man's sin could not ultimately deter him from the fulfillment of God's dream. Jesus came to earth to be our Savior so that God's dream for a family could still be realized. When we receive salvation for our souls by accepting the sacrifice of Jesus, our spirits are born again, and Christ comes to dwell in us with His divine life. Then the Holy Spirit can begin to transform our souls, or personalities, until we become Christlike in our thinking, in our decisions, and in our emotional responses. The better acquainted we become with the Holy Spirit, the more we can expect to be changed into the sons of God with knowledge.

The Personality of the Holy Spirit

The Scriptures reveal the personality of the Holy Spirit in many ways. In the Old Testament the Holy Spirit is present wherever God becomes involved with man. We may not always see the Holy Spirit clearly in these cases, because He is concealed in fourteen emblems that represent different aspects of His Person. (Chapter 3 discusses this topic.) A careful study of the emblems and types that God ordained to represent the Holy Spirit will unfold many aspects of the richness of His divine character and Person. He is typified in many ways in the Old Testament. One of the most beautiful types involves the ingredients of the holy anointing oil that was given to Moses. Understanding the significance of each ingredient reveals a wonderful portrait of the Holy Spirit. For an indepth look at the holy anointing oil and its significance to the Church today, read chapter 1 in the second book in this Holy Spirit series, *Walking in the Anointing of the Holy Spirit.*

The New Testament reveals the Holy Spirit clearly to us, for it records His coming in person to glorify Christ in every believer as He works to create God's family in the earth—that is, the Church. Jesus prepared His disciples for the coming of the Holy Spirit; He taught them many things about His personality. He called the Holy Spirit the *Spirit of Truth*, and *the Counselor* (John 6, NIV). The Holy Spirit can take the truth of the words of Christ, breathe on them, life them, and reveal their depth of meaning to us. He writes the Word of God on the tablets of our hearts until the living Word becomes the Christ life lived in and through us. (See Jeremiah 31:33; 2 Corinthians 3:3.) He is the Comforter who not only comforts us in our earthly sorrows, but also brings a peace into our hearts that the world cannot give.

Although the world defines peace as an absence of hostilities, the peace that the Holy Spirit brings does not depend on circumstances. Real peace is not based on happenings, but on a relationship with the Prince of Peace. When we do not walk in the peace of God, we do not walk in the Spirit. If we find ourselves venting anger, strife, and criticism, that is evidence that we are not walking in harmony with the Person of the Holy Spirit. As we discover life in the Spirit, we learn to walk in truth, peace, grace, and holiness. Each of these virtues is a part of the divine life the Holy Spirit gives.

Jesus taught that truth, comfort, and peace characterize the personality of the Holy Spirit. He also taught that gentleness and patience are divine attributes of the Holy Spirit. It is especially interesting that the Holy Spirit was present at Jesus' baptism in the form of a dove. The predestined plan and purpose of God for symbolizing the Holy Spirit as a dove was to reveal to us the gentle nature of the Holy Spirit. The gentleness of a dove characterizes the personality of the Holy Spirit. He is never harsh, rude, critical, or judgmental. He will convict, correct, instruct, teach, and lead, always in the patient gentleness of His divine personality.

The few characteristics of the personality of the Holy Spirit we have described here should help to establish in our minds that He is a Person. Our goal is to become intimately related to this wonderful Third Person of the Godhead. His purpose is for us to become the expression of God in the earth as we yield our minds, wills, and emotions to the Holy Spirit. As we allow the Holy Spirit to fill us with His divine love, we become God-centered instead of self-centered. Then we begin to know the meaning of life and to fulfill the purposes of God in the living of our lives.

How Can We Relate to the Holy Spirit?

God's ultimate desire is for all His children to know Him through true fellowship and communion in the Holy Spirit. The beauty of His Person as we have briefly described Him should create in us a desire to know Him for the Person He is. My intent is simply to recount the wonders of God as seen in the Person of the Holy Spirit so we might be inspired to acquaint ourselves personally with Him. Paul declared, "I count all things to be loss in view of the surpassing value of knowing Christ Jesus my Lord" (Phil. 3:8, NAS). The Holy Spirit has been given to us so we might know Christ. Jesus said He would send a Comforter, the Holy Spirit, who "shall take of mine, and shall shew it unto you" (John 16:15). It is clear from what Jesus said that we need to know the Holy Spirit intimately in order to enjoy the kind of relationship with God that He intends for His children to enjoy.

The difficulty

Many Christians seem to have some difficulty in coming into the fullness of relationship with the Holy Spirit that the Scriptures teach we can have. Therefore, it will be helpful to briefly examine the causes of this difficulty so that we can overcome it. As I explained more fully in my book *God's Dream,* there are three main reasons behind our lack of relationship with the Holy Spirit as a Person.[1]

First, we have misinterpreted the scripture that says, "Howbeit when he, the Spirit of truth, is come, he will guide you into all truth: for he shall not speak of himself" (John 16:13). We have interpreted this verse to mean that the Holy Spirit did not speak about Himself, that He drew no attention to Himself. Therefore, we have mistakenly concluded that we should not focus our attention on Him either. Although it is true that He came to exalt Jesus, the Holy Spirit, as the Author of the Scriptures, still refers to Himself more than two hundred times in them. So we must have misunderstood the meaning of "He shall not speak of Himself." The more accurate understanding of that phrase is that the Holy Spirit does not speak out of His own resources, but speaks what He hears the Father speak. Because we misinterpreted that verse, we have often deemphasized the importance of relating to the Holy Spirit as the Third Person of the Godhead.

A further difficulty to our coming into relationship with the Holy Spirit is our lack of a reference point for relating to a spiritual being. We can relate in our thinking to God the Father because we have earthly fathers who give us a concept of fatherhood. We identify quite easily with Jesus, since He became a man like us and lived among us. On the other hand, we have no human counterpart for the Holy Spirit, so we have difficulty with His lack of corporeality. We cannot see Him as an entity, nor relate to Him in a human framework. We can begin to overcome this difficulty though, when we learn to see the Holy Spirit in the Church, which is His body on earth.

Each believer becomes a temple of the Holy Spirit, reflecting His character and nature. Paul instructs us on how the body of Christ functions:

> But speaking the truth in love, [you] may grow up into him in all things, which is the head, even Christ: from whom the whole body fitly joined together and compacted by that which every joint supplieth, according to the effectual working in the measure of every part, maketh increase of the body unto the edifying of itself in love.
>
> —Ephesians 4:15–16

Since we are temples of the Holy Spirit, when we learn to be filled with the Holy Spirit individually, we will manifest His life on earth corporately as the body of Christ.

Third, because we have difficulty with His lack of corporeality, we have tried to understand the Holy Spirit solely through emblems that represent Him or through gifts that He bestows. The Holy Spirit is not wind or oil or rain. The Scriptures use these metaphors merely to describe aspects of His Person for us. He is not an "it" or a "tongue" or an influence. He is the Third Person of the Godhead. When we accept the reality of the Holy Spirit being a divine Person, we can learn to respond to Him as the Person He is.

The way to intimacy: personal communion

Once we have accepted the Holy Spirit as a divine Person, we can begin to acquaint ourselves with Him. We can learn to enjoy intimate communion with the Holy Spirit as we give ourselves to prayer and fellowship with Him. We cannot develop a relationship with Him that enables us to walk in the Spirit without cultivating a life of prayer and communion with the Holy Spirit. Although we may sense the blessing of the Holy Spirit as we read the Word and receive His direction in witnessing for Christ, we still may not be truly walking in the Spirit because we lack communion with Him. He can even anoint us as we preach the Word, and give us understanding and discernment of spiritual things, without our walking in the fellowship with Him He had intended. As we discuss more thoroughly the scriptural meaning of "life in the Spirit" (see the second book of this series), we will discover the depth of relationship with the Holy Spirit that is available to believers.

Many of us who have been born again and filled with the Holy Spirit still think of His coming into our lives merely as an experience of power that brought spiritual gifts. In reality, the Holy Spirit comes into our lives as a Person, not as an experience. Getting to know the Holy Spirit requires spending time with Him, allowing Him to talk to us. As we do, we learn to become sensitive to His moods, which reveal His desires in a particular situation or for a particular person. Then He will pray the will of the Father through us for His Church, individually and corporately. And we will learn what pleases Him in even the small issues of our everyday lives.

Results of communion with the Holy Spirit

Victory. Fellowship with the Holy Spirit makes it possible for us to live our daily lives in a way that pleases God. If in the morning we sense His freshness in our hearts, we can gain the strength we need to go through the challenges of that day, knowing that in every situation we will be completely victorious. Perhaps many have discovered, as I have, that we are not smart enough to solve the countless problems we continually face. As we develop a personal communion with the Holy Spirit, we can pray, "Holy Spirit, please lead me and teach me about this problem I am having. Give me Your answer from the mind of God." Then, with assurance, we can await the answer of the Holy Spirit who is faithful to answer and show us the way to victory.

Revelation. Much of the time we spend in prayer with God each day should be devoted to meditating quietly on the Word and allowing the Holy Spirit to speak to our hearts. Revelation comes from the Holy Spirit, who dwells within us. Each time God gives us fresh insight into the Word, He makes the *logos* (the written Word) become a *rhema* (a living Word) to our spirits. Just as the Holy Spirit caused Mary to conceive in her physical body, so the Holy Spirit can impregnate our spirits with the living Word. Reading the Scriptures in communion with the Holy Spirit, who is their Author, causes them to live in our spirits. Spiritual, mental, and physical renewal come to us because we wait in prayer on the Holy Spirit. The Holy Spirit transforms our minds to think God's thoughts, and we come into harmony with the will of God. It is the Holy Spirit who then anoints us to minister with power and authority that revealed Word of God to others.

Protection. Through our fellowship with the Holy Spirit, we receive His protection from the enemy. Many times the persecutions that come from the world do not wound us as deeply as the attacks that come from God's people. Our daily communion with the Holy Spirit can shield us, perhaps not from the actual attacks, but from the negative effects of those attacks. He enables us to come through our fiery trials, not as bitter people, but as better people.

Anointing. The anointing of the Holy Spirit for ministry comes to us through prayer and communion with Him as well. By yielding to Him in obedience and faith, He enables us to exercise the gifts of the Spirit (1 Tim. 4:14–15). Even many who know about the gifts and manifestations of the Spirit do not know how to best operate in them. Paul wrote, "Now concerning spiritual gifts, brethren, I would not have you ignorant" (1 Cor. 12:1). We gain the understanding of spiritual gifts that we need as we fellowship with the Holy Spirit.

Motivation. Even the right heart motivation for exercising the gifts is a result of communion with the Holy Spirit. The apostle Paul taught that the proper motivation for exercising the gifts of the Spirit is love—love for God and for each other (1 Cor. 13). Some teach that love is the greatest gift. That is not what Paul taught. He said to "covet earnestly the best gifts: and yet shew I unto you a more excellent way" (1 Cor. 12:31). Love is not a gift, but a way. Fellowship with the Holy Spirit develops in us the way of love, which keeps all spiritual gifts and manifestations in proper order. Prayer causes individuals' gifts of ministry to work together in harmony, motivated by love and without unhealthy competition.

Ministry. Similarly, the fivefold ministry, given "for the equipping of the saints for the work of service" (Eph. 4:12, NAS), must be released through the anointing of the Holy Spirit that comes through much meditation and prayer. Growth and development in ministry come through waiting on that ministry in prayer and fellowship with the Holy Spirit. Of course, the Holy Spirit administers the fivefold ministry gifts according to the Father's choice. Yet every Spirit-filled person can minister the life of the Holy Spirit. Whether or not you are an apostle, prophet, pastor, teacher, church administrator, elder, or deacon, your spiritual gift will grow and develop to properly edify the body only through prayer and meditation in the Word.

Boldness. The Holy Spirit is God's provision to increase our boldness, inspire our obedience, and strengthen our faith. Obedience to the way He guides us often requires a courage that only prayerful communion and fellowship with the Holy Spirit can produce. Out of communion come the necessary boldness and faith to obey God's Word, for the Holy Spirit believes everything our Lord says. The key to abundant, victorious living is obedience to the Spirit of God. We cannot enjoy the quality of life Jesus came to give to us in abundance without obeying the Holy Spirit. Fellowship with Him strengthens our desire to obey Him. The Christian life can become dull, routine, and even negative if we don't enjoy consistent communion with the Holy Spirit.

Fellowship with the Holy Spirit becomes a way of life for the believer who learns to cultivate a personal relationship with Him. If you are not yet accustomed to this divine relationship with the Holy Spirit, but would like to be, you can simply ask Him to come and make the presence of Christ real to you. Ask Him to give you a new understanding of His Word and to bring you into a new walk of fellowship with Himself. God delights to answer these requests, for they fulfill His will for us. We can learn to walk in a fellowship with the Holy Spirit that will continue to develop all our lives. It will bring us to the maturity that God intended for us to know and experience, thus making us sons of God with knowledge.

God has revealed all we need to know about the Holy Spirit in His Word. As we give ourselves to prayerful study of the Scriptures, we can expect to come into a more satisfying relationship with Him. When we invite Him to come into our lives, He comes to be our Counselor to guide us into all truth. In learning to walk with Him, we can know Him and love Him for the wonderful Person that He is. God intended us to commune with the precious Third Person of the Godhead in order to experience the full redemption of our souls. By becoming more sensitive to the Holy Spirit, we can obey Him more fully and so realize the fulfillment of God's promises in our lives. Then we will come to know His mind, the way He thinks about life. We will discover His will and become a part of it, surrendering our wills in the process. We will recognize

His emotional responses and begin to give correct emotional responses to Him as we learn what pleases and displeases Him.

Even now this beautiful Third Person of the Godhead is waiting for us to seek Him with all of our hearts. Only as we seek Him will we discover the true meaning and purpose of life in God.

CHAPTER

2

Emotional Responses of the Holy Spirit

I would hate to live life without expressing emotion. To some people, expressing emotion is a sign of psychological imbalance, a display of weakness. They especially condemn emotion related to a religious experience. Although they declare it unhealthy to express emotion in religious experiences, these same people think nothing of getting angry with someone or of expressing delight when they receive a gift. They often will make themselves hoarse from yelling excitedly at a ball game. Yet they feel justified in condemning emotional responses in religion. Weeping in prayer or rejoicing in songs of praise would be unacceptable behavior to them.

Some of these people also think it is unmanly to cry.

However, psychologists and medical doctors disagree with that idea. They say that it is not healthy to bottle up our tears inside us. Pent-up emotion becomes poisonous to the health of men and women alike, both mentally and physically. Of course, we cannot ascribe to the philosophy that is prevalent today to "let them have it." Scripture does not advocate our venting anger and other negative emotions irresponsibly. It teaches us, instead, to develop self-control in our lives by yielding to the power of the Holy Spirit. Then we can overcome negative emotional responses. By "pent-up emotion" we refer to the repression of legitimate expressions of emotion as taught in the Word. Emotional health results from freely and correctly responding in each situation with our emotions as they are energized by the Holy Spirit.

Repressing emotion is not a sign of strength but of stubbornness and selfishness. A hardhearted, self-centered person will not express emotions of gratitude or tenderness to God or to others. A man who is happy, complimentary, loving, and tender reflects godly character, not weakness. We need to learn to express emotions honestly and properly, as God intended. When we realize that our emotions constitute one third of our soul (the other two parts being intellect and volition), we begin to better understand their importance to our health and happiness.

The Holy Spirit is a Person who has definite emotional responses, as clearly described in the Scriptures.[1] He is God, and God is love (1 John 4:8). There is no stronger emotion than love. The strength of God's love is most clearly revealed in His willingness to undergo extreme suffering to rescue the object of His love: mankind. The Bible teaches, "For God so loved the world, that he gave his only begotten Son, that whosoever believeth in him should not perish, but have everlasting life" (John 3:16). It was because of His love for mankind that Jesus came to suffer and die on the cross to satisfy the justice of God toward sin. Although hate and anger have wrecked havoc through man's history, the whole universe will one day testify to the supremacy of love. The end of time will culminate in a reign of divine love. The strength of godly love will always be expressed, as it was through Jesus, in sacrificial acts of giving. The love of the Godhead endured the pain of the crucified Savior who gave His life for mankind. Today God still suffers the rejection of men and women who refuse to accept His love. As the Third Person of the Godhead, the Holy Spirit reveals the loving emotions of God. This intense love keeps Him seeking to save those who are lost and rejoicing with the angels when one sinner repents (Luke 15:10; 19:10).

It is incredible to think that human beings have the ability to refuse such divine love. As this divine Personality, the Holy Spirit, seeks to redeem our fallen human personality, we can choose to respond positively or negatively to Him. In human relationships, a positive action toward a person usually evokes a positive response. It is also true that our negative responses to people predictably bring unpleasant consequences. Similarly, the way we respond to the Holy Spirit either builds a loving relationship with Him or hinders the development of that relationship. Of course, the Holy Spirit will always be true to His nature of love. He does not abandon us as people whom we have offended might. He will continue to work in our lives to draw us into a relationship so we can be transformed into the image of Christ. On the other hand, He will never coerce us against our wills, for that would violate the meaning of relationship. *He desires a love response that we choose to give to Him who first loved us.* Our choices affect our fellowship with God just as they do with people. Satisfactory relationships with people depend largely on our responses to them. Our relationship to the Third Person of the Godhead is no exception to that principle.

Negative Responses

Scripture is full of examples and instruction regarding the emotional responses of the Holy Spirit. He responds to sin as God, who cannot tolerate it. He responds to mankind in the long-suffering, entreating way that the love of God uses to seek and to save sinners. He responds to the believer's worship and praise in one way, and to his disobedience in another. The Holy Spirit not only desires to respond to the believer, but also to express Himself through him. Paul taught that "the love of God has been poured out within our hearts through the Holy Spirit who was given to us" (Rom. 5:5, NAS). As we give Him our hearts, He will express the love of God through our lives. Thus, examining the emotional responses of the Holy Spirit that the Scriptures reveal to us will help us better understand this beautiful Third Person of the Godhead.

Grieved

First of all, the Scriptures teach that the Holy Spirit can be grieved. Paul exhorted the Ephesians, "And grieve not the holy Spirit of God, whereby ye are sealed unto the day of redemption" (Eph. 4:30). In this passage, Paul lists such sins as corrupt communications, stealing, lying, bitterness, wrath, and evil speaking, and instructs us to avoid these sins. We can safely conclude that if we do not follow these instructions and repent of these sins, we will grieve the Holy Spirit. We need to understand that because He is love, whatever we do to sin against that love causes Him grief.

Rejection, rebellion, hardness of heart, disobedience, and lack of faith are sinful attitudes of the heart and mind that grieve the Holy Spirit. Sin is conceived in the mind before it becomes a deed. The Scriptures teach that "the heart is deceitful above all things, and desperately wicked: who can know it?" (Jer. 17:9). Jesus said that out of the heart proceeds "evil thoughts, murders, adulteries, fornications, thefts, false witness, blasphemies" (Matt. 15:19). The Holy Spirit alone can change our sinful hearts as we yield to Him. By continually surrendering to Him in obedience, we will live in right relationship with Him so that we do not grieve His heart of love through our thoughts, words, or attitudes and actions.

Vexed

The Scriptures also teach that the Holy Spirit can be vexed. The prophet Isaiah declared, "But they rebelled, and vexed his holy Spirit: therefore he was turned to be their enemy, and he fought against them" (Isa. 63:10). To vex someone means to trouble and bring distress or agitation. The people of Israel vexed the Holy Spirit when they rebelled against His ways. Rebellion against God will always produce negative consequences.

Failing to heed the conviction of the Holy Spirit will finally result in the judgment of God coming into our lives. Yet even in judgment God reveals the strength of His great love, for His intent is always redemptive, never destructive. He uses His judgments to bring us back to Himself with new desires to live in His will and to please Him. The psalmist understood this truth when he wrote, "Before I was afflicted I went astray, but now I keep Thy word....It is good for me that I was afflicted, that I may learn Thy statutes" (Ps. 119:67, 71, NAS). Although affliction is not always a result of disobedience, when affliction comes, we would still be wise to consider our ways. If the Holy Spirit convicts us of sin, and we turn from our rebellion, we can be assured that He will be there to receive our repentance and cleanse us of our sin. If we persist in our sin, we will be sure to vex the precious Holy Spirit and forfeit the peace of God that He brings to those who walk in obedience to Him.

Offended

As we have mentioned, the dove that descended upon Jesus at His baptism was representative of the Holy Spirit (Luke 3:22). That gentle, dove-like nature can be offended. The Holy Spirit is God, and God is love. Therefore, though the Holy Spirit will never react in an unloving way Himself, our unloving responses to Him can offend Him.

In human relationships we are sometimes offended because we are self-centered and "wear our feelings on our sleeves." Becoming easily offended is a carnal reaction, and we need to repent of that. The closer we walk to God, however, the more sensitive we become to His presence, His love, and His nature. A closer walk also sensitizes us to anything that is incompatible to His nature. Our awareness of harshness, unkindness, and rudeness in people will be greater compared to our awareness of the loving presence of God. Though our responses to such negative attitudes may be more godly, we will feel more deeply the "unlove" of people when we have been communing with the love of God. If that is true in our limited human experience, what must the Holy Spirit, who is pure love, feel when He encounters our unloving attitudes?

Offending one of our brothers or sisters in Christ, our spouse, or our children, hurts the heart of the Holy Spirit, for He dwells in each of them. Paul exhorted the Ephesian Christians to "be kind to one another, tenderhearted, forgiving each other, just as God in Christ also has forgiven you" (Eph. 4:32, NAS). His instructions are very clear about how we are to treat one another as Christians. We are expected to respond to each other "with all humility and gentleness, with patience, showing forbearance to one another in love, being diligent to preserve the unity of the Spirit in the bond of peace" (Eph. 4:2–3, NAS). These attitudes are not natural to our human nature. Only the Holy Spirit can work them into our hearts as He fills us with

His love for the brethren. When we offend the Holy Spirit by sinning against a person, even unintentionally, we need to repent for our sin against God's love.

Quenched

As a gentle Person, the Holy Spirit does not insist, against our wills, that we obey Him. He waits to be invited and welcomed into our lives. Then He patiently persuades us of truth and righteousness. The Scriptures teach us to "quench not the Spirit" (1 Thess. 5:19). If we do not choose to obey the Holy Spirit, we will quench His work in our lives. The word picture in the Greek for quenching the Spirit is literally "choking the throat of the Holy Spirit." One way we can do that is by refusing to heed His convicting word to our hearts about our sin. As individual believers, we can expect the Holy Spirit to speak truth to us about our lives. It is imperative that we yield to His gentle but clear leading as He desires to counsel us and lead us into all truth. If we do not, we may be guilty of quenching His presence in our lives. In that case, we are left with our sin nature in control until we choose to repent and allow the Holy Spirit to govern us again.

We must understand that it is possible to quench the moving of the Holy Spirit as church bodies also. We need to become sensitive to the Holy Spirit's desires for our worship services. For example, some churches have become embarrassed by the moving of the Holy Spirit through the gifts of tongues and interpretation. They relegate such "interruptions" to the prayer room on Wednesday nights. Other church programs leave no room for the Holy Spirit to change the agendas that their leaders judiciously control. Yielding to the Holy Spirit in faith, without knowing exactly how He will move, creates an uncertainty in their minds that they are unwilling to allow. They would rather quench the life flow of the Holy Spirit than to lose "control" of the meeting. Such attitudes hinder our corporate relationship to the Holy Spirit in the body of Christ by quenching His moving. To follow the Holy Spirit's guidance as He teaches us to worship requires cultivating a sensitive relationship to Him. As we do, we can avoid quenching His moving and enjoy His presence.

Lied to

It is also possible to lie to the Holy Spirit as we would to any other person, but not without consequences. Ananias and Sapphira, people in the early church, lied to the Holy Ghost (Acts 5). Peter knew by the Holy Spirit that they were lying. He rebuked them, asking them why Satan had filled their hearts to lie to the Holy Ghost. They had not lied to men but to God, and they died immediately because of God's judgment upon them. We must be careful when we make vows to God concerning our lives. Our loving heavenly Father is not waiting to pounce on us if we stumble in our commitment or even fail miserably. But if we promise Him one thing while fully intending to do another, we are not lying to men, but to God.

Defrauded

We can defraud the Holy Spirit of His honor by taking to ourselves the honor due Him. The Bible records the fate of two prominent leaders who refused to give God the glory due Him. The Old Testament example is King Nebuchadnezzar of Babylon who gloried in the mighty kingdom he had built by the might of his power and for the honor of his majesty. Because he took credit for his own greatness, he lost his mind and went into the fields to live with the beasts for seven years. When he finally lifted up his eyes to heaven and praised God, his reason returned to him, and he was again established in his kingdom. Then he declared, "Now I Nebuchadnezzar praise and extol and honour the King of heaven, all whose works are truth, and his ways judgment: and those that walk in pride he is able to abase" (Dan. 4:37).

The New Testament records a worse fate for King Herod when he arrayed himself in his royal apparel and gave a grandiose speech to the people. They promptly acclaimed him to be a god. "And immediately the angel of the Lord smote him, because he gave not God the glory: and he was eaten of worms, and gave up the ghost" (Acts 12:23). It is dangerous for anyone to sin against God by breaking the first commandment, "Thou shalt have no other gods before me" (Exod. 20:3). Although we would not blatantly bow down to another god, we need to examine our hearts when we take credit for personal accomplishments instead of giving glory to God, who enables us to succeed.

When God gives us revelation in the Word and we share it with others, we dare not take credit for the blessing it brings to peoples' lives. It is the Holy Spirit who gives us the ability to understand the Word. We must be careful to acknowledge Him and give Him the glory for opening the truth to us. Similarly, when we have grace to give financially into the kingdom, we need to guard against becoming conceited, as though we were doing a great thing. It is a work of the Holy Spirit in our selfish human nature that enables us to be generous, cheerful givers. We are not basically good, as the secular humanist insists. We are dependent on the Holy Spirit to enable us to live in a way that pleases God in every area of our lives. We must be careful not to defraud the Holy Spirit by taking glory to ourselves as though we are responsible for what He is doing in us to redeem us.

Resisted

Peter preached to the Jews on the Day of Pentecost, rebuking them as "stiffnecked and uncircumcised in heart and ears" who "always resist the Holy Ghost" (Acts 7:51). It is incredible to think that we finite human beings have the dubious power of resisting the plans and purposes the Third Person of the Godhead has for us. Yet, when the gentle Holy Spirit comes to bring conviction to our hearts and we do not repent of our sin, we are guilty of resisting Him, and we remain in our sin. His divine purpose is to continually cleanse us and change us into the image of Christ. As Christians, we can expect the Holy Spirit to teach us the truth from the Word and to lead and guide us into all the will of God for our lives if we do not resist Him.

Blasphemed

Finally, we must not omit the awful fact that it is possible for us to blaspheme the Holy Spirit. A simple definition of *blasphemy against the Holy Spirit* is to "deliberately and willfully attribute the work of the Holy Spirit to the devil."

The context of Jesus' teaching about this subject was the critical, defiant attitude of the Pharisees regarding His work of exorcising evil spirits. They kept accusing Christ of casting out demons by the power and authority of Beelzebub....Specifically, therefore, the Pharisees were blaspheming or slandering the Holy Spirit by giving the devil credit for Jesus' miracles of exorcism, when in reality these were wrought by the Spirit of God. But this false accusation was merely symptomatic of the underlying sin for which there is no forgiveness (Matt. 12:33–37). Their words would condemn them, for these evidenced a fixed, unrepentant attitude of mind that persistently rejected the wooing and conviction of the Spirit.[2]

Satan tries to frighten and condemn people with the threat that they have committed the unpardonable sin. No one is in danger of committing the sin of blasphemy against the Holy Spirit *unless* he has known God and then willfully turned from God in disobedience and rejection of Him. A hardened heart and a stiff neck of disobedience lead to a state of apostasy that can result in blasphemy (Jer. 10:26–31). If a person desires to be forgiven for sin, that is evidence that he does not have a heart that has committed the unpardonable sin of blasphemy against the Holy Spirit. God *always* forgives a repentant sinner if he turns from his sin and desires to be forgiven. It is comforting to know that if we are concerned about our sin, we are not in that unrepentant state of hardheartedness that results in apostasy and blasphemy. We need only rebuke Satan's lie and repent of our sin to come into peace and relationship with the Holy Spirit.

If we are aware that we can displease the Holy Spirit in these ways, then we can guard against them and learn to please Him in all our responses to life. In cultivating a relationship with the Holy Spirit, unlike some of our relationships with people, we can be assured of His loving response to us. He will even enable us to respond lovingly to unloving people as we allow Him to live the life of Christ through us.

Positive Responses

Obeyed

If our disobedience grieves the Holy Spirit, then we can be assured that our obedience delights His heart. As we yield to His convicting power and obey His truth as He reveals it to us, we will begin to know the righteousness, peace, and joy of the Holy Ghost in our lives and churches. The psalmist declared, "Thy word is a lamp to my feet, and a light to my path" (Ps. 119:105, NAS). Walking in obedience to the Word of God helps us become properly related to the Holy Spirit. Not only will our individual lives bring glory to God, but we also will enjoy His presence corporately in our churches as we walk in His precepts, obeying His commands with joy.

Believed

The Holy Spirit is the Spirit of Truth. We must respond positively to the truth He reveals by choosing to believe Him if we are to experience His divine power in setting us free from sin. Paul wrote to the church at Thessalonica that they were chosen "to salvation through sanctification of the Spirit and belief of the truth" (2 Thess. 2:13). Our salvation is not possible without our first believing the Spirit of Truth.

It is a true maxim that we live what we believe. If we believe that money is the most important thing in this life, we will spend all our energies in pursuing it. If we believe that obedience to God is the one great priority that will bring true success, then we will yield to the Holy Spirit and obey the Word of God. Actually, yielding to the Holy Spirit is not an option for the Christian; it is a command. Paul instructs believers to "yield yourselves unto God, as those that are alive from the dead, and your members as instruments of righteousness unto God. For sin shall not have dominion over you" (Rom. 6:13–14). Obedience is a result of our yielding our wills to the will of the Holy Spirit.

All the promises of God belong to those who cheerfully obey the will of God revealed through the Word of God by the Holy Spirit. The Holy Spirit not only teaches us how to obey, but also gives us the desire and the power to do so as we walk in relationship with Him. Paul encouraged the Philippians:

> Wherefore, my beloved, as ye have always
> obeyed, not as in my presence only, but now

much more in my absence, work out your own salvation with fear and trembling. For it is God which worketh in you both to will and to do of his good pleasure.

—PHILIPPIANS 2:12–13

Only the power of the Holy Spirit can change a human heart from its natural bent toward sin and fill it with a delight in doing the will of God. That is why our relationship with the Holy Spirit is so imperative; we cannot obey God otherwise.

Honored

Giving honor is a prerequisite for having healthy relationships. We hear much teaching today about how to give honor in all our relationships with both family and friends. *Honor* is defined as "the esteem and respect bestowed on a person." The Holy Spirit teaches us how to honor God first and then how to bring that attitude to all our other relationships. We honor the Holy Spirit by acknowledging Him in all our ways, looking to Him as our Counselor, Comforter, and divine Guide into all truth. He is honored when we esteem the Word of God and obey it. Paul instructed Christians, "In lowliness of mind let each esteem other better than themselves" (Phil. 2:3). As the humility of Christ is worked into our relationships with one another, we honor one another as well as God.

This wonderful Third Person of the Godhead can make our lives victorious as we learn to hear and obey Him in all things. It is our responsibility to respond properly to Him by yielding to Him in obedience, by believing Him, and by honoring Him in the living of our lives. We need to realize that we are responding to a Person, not to an influence or an "it." His loving response to us will encourage us to strengthen our relationship with Him. As we mature in our walk with God, we can know the true heart satisfaction in relating to the Holy Spirit as a Person and by enjoying His response to us as beloved children of God.

The beauties of this Third Person of the Godhead have been typified throughout the Scriptures to illustrate for us His infinite majesty. As we continue to study His Personhood, we will discover His beauty in many of the Old Testament pictures or emblems of the Holy Spirit. We will learn to recognize many divine aspects of His personality in each of these eternal portraits.

3

Emblems Reveal the Holy Spirit's Character

Many of God's dear teachers, ministers, and students seem to have the mistaken idea that the study of emblems and types found in the Scriptures is fanciful and farfetched or, at best, of very little importance. The fact is, types and shadows that tell of future realities run through the entire Book and contain untold wealth for the reverent student who is willing to become a miner of the hidden treasures of God's Holy Word.

In the Book of Moses and the historical books there are many typical characters, events, and institutions. In the poetical books, we have

> typical utterances by typical characters. In the prophecies, we again have typical characters and events where the fulfillment of types is foretold, while throughout the New Testament they are constantly referred to and explained and the great anti-type is presented.[1]

It is important for us to clearly understand what we mean by a "type." A type prefigures, or symbolizes, something or someone. It is a person, place, thing, event, or incident that is recorded in the Bible to teach us spiritual lessons and to open to us some truths about God or His people. These persons and places were not mythical; they were actual historical facts. The typical events recorded in the Scriptures really happened; they are not mere allegories. But they each convey a truth in type that is larger than the natural realities they represent.

We should always be careful not to set forth anything as a type that the Scriptures themselves do not so designate. But if we dig deeply enough, we shall find that almost every incident in the Old Testament history that is referred to in the New Testament has been *typical* in its teaching. This becomes especially clear when we remember that the apostle Paul, after summing up the main events of Israel's history, wrote: "Now all these things happened unto them for ensamples [types]: and they are written for our admonition, upon whom the ends of the world are come" (1 Cor. 10:11). Let us bear this great statement in mind as we proceed to study the types and emblems of the Holy Spirit.

Old Testament types may be compared to *pictures* in a beautifully illustrated book. The New Testament can be compared to the *captions* in that book that explain the pictures of the Old Testament. If we were to read the captions in a book without ever looking at the pictures to which they refer, we would miss much of the book's inspiration as well as find it much more difficult to understand. In the same way we Christians lose great blessings and inspiration if we study only the New Testament and try to comprehend its deep truths without referring to the Old Testament, where those very truths are set forth in types and emblems that make them easier to understand.

An *emblem* represents, metaphorically, an abstract idea or an invisible element and helps to define its general ethical or spiritual meaning.[2] There are at least fourteen emblems used in the Scripture to represent various aspects of the Holy Spirit. Each emblem reveals a beautiful facet of the Holy Spirit's nature and of His work on earth. Of course, this divine Personality can be truly understood only by the revelation of Himself to our hearts. But just as similes and metaphors give our minds a picture to grasp, so types and emblems help to open our understanding to the revelation of His Person.

Why are there so many types and emblems in the Scriptures? It is because the beauty of our glorious Savior is so transcendent, so wonderful, that no single picture could ever express the depth of truth contained in Him. Neither can the infinite beauty of the Holy Spirit be fully revealed through one or two pictures or emblems. That is why we find so many pictures of the Holy Spirit in the Old

Testament. When there is repetition in some illustrations of the Holy Spirit, it is because our heavenly Father knows our weakness of comprehension and the shortness of our memory. Even so, we shall discover that each picture or emblem illustrates a distinct revelation peculiar to itself.

Often the same object is used, on different occasions, as one type in order to express different spiritual concepts. For example, the serpent is used as a type of the devil (Rev. 12:9). Jesus changes the picture when He uses the serpent as a type of Himself being lifted up on the cross (John 3:14). Then He tells His disciples to be wise as serpents and harmless as doves (Matt. 10:16). In each case the serpent represents a different spiritual reality. The context of the Scripture will make clear to us the use of the type or emblem. As we study in a humble, yielded spirit, looking to the Holy Spirit for guidance at every step, He will not fail to open to us these wonderful treasures of His own Word.

The Dove

The Spirit of God descended on Jesus at His baptism like a dove (Matt. 3:16). It must have been a moving experience for those standing on the river bank that day to see a dove light on Jesus and to hear the voice of God from heaven saying, "This is my beloved Son, in whom I am well pleased" (Matt. 3:17). Although they were not accustomed to witnessing supernatural events, surely they must have thrilled to the presence of God manifested in that hour.

As we mentioned earlier, the gentleness of the dove characterizes the personality of the Holy Spirit. The dove that Noah sent out of the ark became his servant to bring him news of the earth's condition after the flood. In that same way the Holy Spirit is God serving mankind, bringing us to a knowledge of eternal life and filling us with that life at our request. The gentleness and servant spirit of the dove show us the kind of God that is without a hint of harshness or violence. He gently persuades us of the truth of God's love, then waits for us to invite Him into our lives. He will never coerce us to repent or to obey Him. The Holy Spirit will always deal with mankind in a way that is in character with His gentle nature.

Even in our most painful situations, we dare not think that God allowed our difficulties because of any unkindness in Him. He cannot treat us unkindly, for His divine nature is kind and gentle. Jesus said, "Come to Me, all who are weary and heavy-laden, and I will give you rest. Take My yoke upon you, and learn from Me, for I am gentle and humble in heart; and you shall find rest for your souls" (Matt. 11:28–29, NAS). The Spirit of God, who came to reveal Jesus to us, reflects that gentleness in all He does.

The Seal of Promise

Now He who establishes us with you in Christ and anointed us is God, who also sealed us and gave us the Spirit in our hearts as a pledge.
—2 CORINTHIANS 1:21–22, NAS

The purpose of a seal is to ratify and confirm, to give guarantee and assurance of certain claims. Paul taught the Ephesian believers that they were sealed in Christ "with the Holy Spirit of promise, who is given as a pledge of our inheritance" (Eph. 1:13–14, NAS). In this same passage, Paul referred to the believer as "God's own possession." The seal, in this sense, represents the proprietorship of God's love. God has stamped us as His possession, His very own property. This scriptural seal of promise represents the security of the believer and the guarantee that God's promise of eternal life is real. When the devil tries to convince us that we have sinned too terribly to be called Christians, we need to remind him that the Holy Spirit of promise has sealed us. Simply repenting of present sin will bring a cleansing of the blood of Christ, and we can resume fellowship as though we had never sinned. The Word declares, "If we walk in the light, as he is in the light, we have fellowship one with another, and the blood of Jesus Christ his Son cleanseth us from all sin" (1 John 1:7). The seal of promise is a present reality that guarantees our eternal future with God. It is the presence of the Holy Spirit in our lives that reminds us we belong to God and will live eternally with Him.

Act of Anointing

God ordained the act of anointing when He instructed Moses to create the anointing oil. It symbolizes the Holy Spirit's consecrating grace and guidance for the believer. Paul declared that his anointing was from God, "who also sealed us and gave us the Spirit in our hearts as a pledge" (2 Cor. 1:22, NAS). He meant that God has made us like the anointed One, Christ Jesus, in the sense that the same Spirit has anointed both Christ and us.[3] The Scriptures teach us that "the anointing which you received from Him abides in you, and you have no need for anyone to teach you; but as His anointing teaches you about all things, and is true and is not a lie, and just as it has taught you, you abide in Him" (1 John 2:27, NAS). The abiding presence of the Holy Spirit is the anointing that gives believers the capacity to know the truth and to be set free from every form of deception.

It was written of Jesus, "Thou hast loved righteousness, and hated iniquity; therefore God, even thy God, hath anointed thee with the oil of gladness above thy fellows" (Heb. 1:9). Jesus lived His life in complete separation from sin. He consecrated Himself to the Father to do only His will. For that reason, the Father gave Him the Spirit without measure (John 3:34). He was fully consecrated and divinely qualified for ministry through the anointing of the Holy Spirit.

We see the Old Testament counterpart of this consecration experience in the lives of the priests. The holy anointing oil was poured over the heads of Aaron and his sons to consecrate them to the ministry of the priesthood (Exod. 29). As New Testament believers, we are called to be a holy priesthood, "to offer up spiritual sacrifices, acceptable to God by Jesus Christ" (1 Pet. 2:5). The Holy Spirit empowers us to fulfill our priestly calling. It is the anointing of the Holy Spirit that qualifies us for ministry in the same way the anointing oil did, in type, the Old Testament priests.

Oil

A most useful characteristic of oil is the light it provides when it is burned in a lamp. People living in Bible days perhaps appreciated that fact more because oil was the chief source of illumination apart from the sun. That light symbolizes the power of the Holy Spirit to illuminate truth to us. Jesus taught the parable of the wise virgins who took plenty of oil for their lamps and the foolish virgins who did not. The foolish virgins were away buying more oil when the bridegroom came (Matt. 25:1–13). Without the oil of the Spirit being plentiful in our lives, we will not be ready when the Bridegroom comes. We must "buy the truth, and sell it not" (Prov. 23:23), and allow the Holy Spirit to teach us all things so we will be prepared for the coming of the Lord.

Jesus said, "I am the light of the world" (John 8:12). The Holy Spirit filled Him, and He walked as light in the darkness of this world. Then He declared to His disciples, "Ye are the light of the world" (Matt. 5:14). Only as the Holy Spirit fills our lives can we have truth illumined to us. Then we can become light to the darkened minds of men who do not know God.

Fire

Many times the Scriptures refer to fire to typify the presence of God. When the children of Israel were in the wilderness, the presence of the Lord was with them in a cloud by day and a pillar of fire by night (Exod. 13:21). Later in history, God declared through His prophet Malachi that the coming of the Lord was like a refiner's fire (Mal. 3:2). John the Baptist preached this:

> He that cometh after me is mightier than I, whose shoes I am not worthy to bear: he shall baptize you with the Holy Ghost, and with fire: whose fan is in his hand, and he will thoroughly purge his floor, and gather his wheat into the garner; but he will burn up the chaff with unquenchable fire.
> —MATTHEW 3:11–12

Why fire? We sometimes fear fire, having seen the devastation it can cause to a home and anything else it touches when it's out of control. Fire has the power to destroy. But that is not the reason God uses fire to represent the Holy Spirit. The work of the Holy Spirit is redemptive, not destructive. When under control, fire is an invaluable element that provides warmth and light and that cleanses and purifies whatever it touches. The Scriptures teach that "our God is a consuming fire" (Heb. 12:29). His holiness is the essence of that fire.

The fire of God that appeared in the cutting of the covenant with Abraham showed God's approval of Abraham's worship (Gen. 15:17). When Elijah called fire down out of heaven on Mount Carmel, it consumed the sacrifice and proved to the Baal worshipers that the Lord was the true God (1 Kings 18:17–40). When we lift our hearts in worship, we should realize we are standing in the presence of a holy God whose fire can consume the sin in our lives. However, there should be no fear of destruction from that divine fire—only an awesome fellowship in the presence of a holy God.

As our lives are cleansed by fire, so our work will be tried with fire. Everything that is not of eternal value will be burned. We will not need a bonfire to try our works and consume all that is wood, hay, and stubble. The very presence of God, the Consuming Fire before whom we will give account of the deeds done, will consume all that are works of flesh and our fleshly programs. Paul declared, "Each man's work will become evident; for the day will show it, because it is to be revealed with fire; and the fire itself will test the quality of each man's work" (1 Cor. 3:13, NAS). Our motivation, our faithfulness, and our attitudes will be exposed to the light of the fire of His holiness.

The fire of God is a place of safety and security for the believer; it saves us from deception and uncleanness. It is there we can enjoy the light that casts out the darkness. To walk in the fire results in forgiveness, health, and stability. As temples of the Holy Ghost, we believers need to be continually cleansed, forgiven, and made whole. The Holy Spirit comes as fire to cleanse our temples and to make us holy as He is holy.

Rain

The Scriptures refer to the outpouring of the Holy Spirit as the early and latter rains. "Then shall we know, if we follow on to know the LORD: his going forth is prepared as the morning; and he shall come unto us as the rain, as the latter and former rain unto the earth" (Hos. 6:3). To a farmer, the latter rains are as equally important as the early rains for the maturing of the harvest. As a faithful husbandman, God watches over His harvest. "Behold, the husbandman waiteth for the precious fruit of the earth, and hath long patience for it, until he receive the early and latter rain" (James 5:7). God is not building His Church in a day. He is patiently working by His Spirit until we grow into maturity to become a glorious Church without spot or wrinkle. The life-giving rain that typifies the moving of the Holy Spirit is vital to that growth.

Rain speaks of the abundance of the Spirit's supply. The latter rain will bring an abundance of God's presence. "He shall come down like rain upon the mown grass: as showers that water the earth. In his days shall the righteous flourish; and abundance of peace so long as the moon endureth" (Ps. 72:6–7). We live in anticipation of the coming of the Holy Spirit to our hearts and to His Church as life-giving rain.

Breath (Air)

The word for *spirit* in the Greek language is *pneuma*. It means "breath." Breath is the element that depicts the Holy Spirit's exclusiveness. In the new birth experience, the Holy Spirit breathes the life of God into our spirits, causing us to live unto God. Thus, that life-giving breath belongs only to those who have been born again. God sent the Holy Ghost to the Church, not to the world. He convicts the world of sin, but He came to the Church to reveal Christ to her and to prepare her to live with the Father.

The difference between the man who has only immortal life and the one who has both immortal life and the quickened spirit is his destiny. The first will live forever without God; the latter will live forever in the presence of God. The breath of the Holy Spirit gives life to our spirits when we are born again by the Spirit, when we accept the sacrifice of Jesus' blood for the forgiveness of our sins. He implants His seed (the Word) into our spirits and breathes His life into us, and we become children of God with eternal life. Christ is eternal life. If we have Christ living in us, we have life. Without Christ, we do not have life. We cannot live in God without the breath of God quickening our spirits.

Wind

There are instances in both the Old and New Testaments where wind typifies the moving of the Holy Spirit. When Ezekiel found himself in the valley of dry bones, God told him to prophesy to the wind and say, "Come from the four winds, O breath, and breathe upon these slain, that they may live" (Ezek. 37:9). When the breath came into them, they lived and stood up as a great army. The picture of the wind that brought life to the dead bones is a type of the Holy Spirit who has power to create life within us. When Jesus was explaining salvation to Nicodemus, He said, "The wind bloweth where it listeth" (John 3:8). Jesus told him that we can hear the sound of the wind, but we cannot tell where it came from or where it is going (v. 8). He used the simile of wind to describe the moving of the Holy Spirit.

On the Day of Pentecost, the Holy Spirit descended with the "sound from heaven as of a rushing mighty wind, and it filled all the house where they were sitting" (Acts 2:2). The Holy Spirit is not wind, but His coming was so powerful and awesome that it sounded like a rushing mighty wind to the disciples. This is the only description given in Scripture of the coming of the Holy Spirit on the Day of Pentecost. The disciples' lives were transformed as they experienced the omnipotent power of God in the Third Person of the Godhead coming to them as a mighty wind.

River of God

Jesus declared, "'He who believes in Me, as the Scripture said, "From his innermost being shall flow rivers of living water."' But this He spoke of the Spirit, whom those who believed in Him were to receive" (John 7:38–39, NAS). Jesus referred here to the river as a type to describe the life-giving force of the Holy Spirit. A river is a source of water that sustains life abundantly. The psalmist described the life of a godly man as "a tree planted by the rivers of water, that bringeth forth his fruit in his season;

his leaf also shall not wither; and whatsoever he doeth shall prosper" (Ps. 1:3). This beautiful simile of the fruitful life of the righteous symbolizes the power of the Holy Spirit as a river that continually brings abundant life to believers. When the river of God flows freely in our lives, we will bear fruit for the kingdom, and everything we do will prosper.

Dew

Dew is that refreshing moisture so welcome after the heat of the sun has disappeared. These droplets settle in peace over the land and fill it with delight. The dew falls at night when all the creation is resting and the natural elements are at peace. Dew represents the restfulness in the kingdom of God that the Holy Spirit came to give. When God provided Israel with daily manna in the wilderness, it fell with the dew upon the camp at night (Num. 11:9). Jesus referred to that manna when He proclaimed Himself to be the bread of life (John 6:32–35). In this type, the manna represented Jesus. The dew that fell with the manna symbolized the presence of the Holy Spirit. He will always be present where Jesus is present.

Job described this restful state when he wrote, "My root was spread out by the waters, and the dew lay all night upon my branch. My glory was fresh in me, and my bow was renewed in my hand" (Job 29:19–20). The prophet Isaiah foretold the Holy Spirit's desire to give us rest: "For with stammering lips and another tongue will he speak to this people. To whom he said, This is the rest wherewith ye may cause the weary to rest; and this is the refreshing: yet they would not hear" (Isa. 28:11–12).

The Holy Spirit promises welcome rest not only to the individual believer, but to the corporate body of Christ as well. The psalmist declared, "Behold, how good and how pleasant it is for brethren to dwell together in unity!…As the dew of Hermon, and as the dew that descended upon the mountains of Zion: for there the LORD commanded the blessing, even life for evermore" (Ps. 133:1, 3). Only the Holy Spirit can bring men together in unity in the body of Christ. Unity is like the dew of heaven, full of pleasantness and refreshment. It is in unity that the Lord commands the blessing, the eternal life of the Spirit.

Water

Water is often used as an emblem of the Holy Spirit in the Scriptures, as we have seen in our study of the symbolism of rain, dew, and the river of God. Water is more necessary than food to man's life. We can survive without food for a considerably longer period than we can survive without water. The lack of water reduces life to an arid desert, a land without hope of fruitfulness. God's purpose is fruitfulness for all who receive the Spirit of God. When water symbolizes the Holy Spirit, the picture is always one of abundance, like rivers, springs, and wells that never run dry.

Water from the rock

God gave Moses instructions on how to receive life-giving water out of a rock. "Behold, I will stand before thee there upon the rock in Horeb; and thou shalt smite the rock, and there shall come water out of it, that the people may drink. And Moses did so in the sight of the elders of Israel" (Exod. 17:6). The miracle of receiving water out of a rock beautifully typifies for us the power of the Holy Spirit flowing out of Christ, who is our Rock. When Christ gave the Holy Spirit to believers, we received Him as living water out of our Rock, Christ Jesus.

Water springs

When the psalmist cried out, "All my springs are in thee" (Ps. 87:7), he was acknowledging God as the only source of life. Water springs depict the very beginning of the source of life. Mountain springs feed the largest rivers at their starting points, the places where the rain and snows begin their long trek downward to the sea. The story of Caleb's daughter in the Old Testament illustrates the importance of water springs. When Caleb's daughter asked her father for a blessing, she said, "For thou hast given me a south land; give me also springs of water" (Josh. 15:19). She knew the life-giving value of water springs. Her father granted her request. Our Father will grant ours as well when we ask for the power of the Holy Spirit to be our source of life.

We dare not look to any other source for life, which God's people have sometimes done throughout history. Jeremiah voiced God's lament that "my people have committed two evils; they have forsaken me the fountain of living waters, and hewed them out cisterns, broken cisterns, that can hold no water" (Jer. 2:13). Looking for life from any source other than God is like molding broken clay cups that cannot contain refreshing, life-giving water for us.

Wells of salvation

Wells of salvation correspond to the rivers of living water that Jesus said would flow out of our innermost beings. Jesus told the woman at the well, "But whosoever drinketh of the water that I shall give him shall never thirst; but the water that I shall give him shall be in him a well of water springing up into everlasting life" (John 4:14). The Holy Spirit, like the well, has an unlimited supply of life. The prophet Isaiah had this revelation when he declared, "Behold, God is my salvation; I will trust, and not be afraid: for the LORD JEHOVAH is my strength and my song; he also is become my salvation. Therefore with joy shall ye draw water out of the wells of salvation" (Isa. 12:2–3).

Valley of Baca

The valley of Baca represents a place of difficulties and tears. We probably would not think of this valley as a place of blessing. The Scriptures, however, teach:

> Blessed is the man whose strength is in thee; in whose heart are the ways of them. Who passing through the valley of Baca make it a well; the rain also filleth the pools. They go from strength to strength, every one of them in Zion appeareth before God.
>
> —PSALM 84:5–7

As we walk through difficulties in the power of the Holy Spirit, He transforms those problems into a well of life-giving strength for us.

We also can translate the Hebrew word for *well* as "a place of springs." Even our most difficult situations can become a spring, a source of life to us as we discover how to abide in Christ in our suffering, drawing on the strength of the Spirit and experiencing His protection. Pain and suffering do not threaten the life of Christ. On the contrary, they become pathways to new springs of comfort and strength as we call on the Holy Spirit during those times of affliction. We learn to go from strength to strength.

Clothing

When the Scriptures refer to the Spirit clothing individuals, they are describing the power of the Holy Spirit to equip. When God chose to use Gideon, for example, as a deliverer for His people, we read, "But the Spirit of the LORD came upon Gideon, and he blew a trumpet" (Judg. 6:34). This verse can be translated as, "But the Spirit of the Lord clothed Gideon." God equipped Gideon for the task He gave him to do when the Spirit of the Lord came upon him.

Jesus told the disciples to tarry in Jerusalem until they were endued with power from on high at the coming of the Holy Spirit (Luke 24:49). The word *endued* can be translated as "clothed" also. The Holy Spirit clothed the disciples with power to become witnesses to the gospel throughout the world. They were equipped by the Spirit to fulfill the will of God.

Earnest

The word *earnest* in the Greek refers to the first down payment, which assures the recipient of final payment in full. In modern Greek it means an engagement ring, the token of future marriage from the lover to his prospective bride! Paul wrote to the Ephesians, "Ye were sealed with that holy Spirit of promise, which is the earnest of our inheritance until the redemption of the purchased possession" (Eph. 1:13–14). We have not received the fullness of our inheritance yet, but God gave us the Holy Spirit as a sample of what life will be like when we are fully redeemed. He is the down payment of our inheritance in Christ.

A little child slipped into his mother's kitchen where she was mixing a rich batter for a special homemade cake. The child stuck his fingers into that batter and then, licking them as he ran out the door, asked when the cake would be done. Having the Holy Spirit in our lives is like the wonderful taste of batter on our fingers; it makes us anticipate the finished cake. As the Holy Spirit brings us into Christ's presence, He gives us a foretaste of being received as Christ's bride and enjoying everlasting love and communion with Him.

When Paul describes a people of God who are "sealed with that holy Spirit of promise" (Eph. 1:13), he is speaking of the Holy Spirit's work of producing a mark of identification, of ownership, an engraving of a glorious inner work, in His people. The Holy Spirit labels them as God's very own property, accepted by Him. A supernatural work has changed those people forever. They are not ordinary people anymore; they are no longer of this world. They have set their affections on things above, not on things of this earth (Col. 3:2). They are not so taken up, interested in, or participants of this world's events. They are not shaken by every word of doom and gloom that comes along. They are no longer a part of a half-hearted, lukewarm congregation. They know that there is nothing worse than being in a church where God used to be or than in not knowing the purpose for which they were placed on the earth. Their heart cries out, "Even so, come quickly, Lord Jesus."

You might ask, "What happened to change them? What did the Holy Spirit do in that believer? What marked and sealed them forever as the Lord's possession?" It was simply this: the Holy Spirit gave them a foretaste of the glory of His presence. He came to them, opened their spiritual eyes, divided the veil of the flesh, and allowed them to experience a supernatural manifestation of His exceeding greatness. Isn't that why it is so necessary for God's house to be a place of prayer, purity, and power? Is that not what the psalmist was saying when he asked, "Who shall ascend into the hill of the Lord? or who shall stand in his holy place? He that hath clean hands, and a pure heart" (Ps. 24:3–4). That is why we should not allow anything in our lives to hinder the Holy Spirit's work. We need the Spirit of God to pull back the veil of our flesh and give us a foretaste of our inheritance, an earnest of what we will one day receive in full.

God is sealing His people for His purposes in our day. We can go to meetings now where Jesus is so real that we can taste a little bit of heaven in our souls. We come away with the sense of eternal reality, that an eternal work has been done inside of us. We feel we were not just challenged by a sermon, but were changed more into His image. God has put a holy fire in our soul, and there is no more fear of the enemy—the world, the flesh, and the devil. There is a security in knowing that we have received a supernatural touch from God. We leave that service saying, "This isn't me. This is God's Spirit working inside of me."

You may have heard it said that God gives us a little heaven to go to heaven in. I used to wonder what that meant. Now I think it simply means that He whets our appetite by letting us look into the glory of His kingdom. We get a taste of His holiness, His love, His rest, and His peace. Then we are forever spoiled for this world because we have had a taste. Now we yearn for the fullness—or the cake, if you please—that we have only tasted. The Holy Spirit is the earnest of that fullness.

Summary

These emblems, taken together, provide a beautiful and comforting portrait of the Holy Spirit. The Holy Spirit is not an emblem. As the Third Person of the Godhead, He is a very desirable, divine Person. However, the life-giving qualities of these emblems accurately reveal to us many characteristics of this beautiful Third Person of the Godhead, as well as His lovely character and His great power to redeem the sons of men. These emblems show us His great desire to give abundant life to all who will receive Him.

CHAPTER

4

Sevenfold Power of the Holy Spirit
The Omnipotence of God Revealed

In order to speak comprehensively of the power of the Holy Spirit, we need to define *divine omnipotence* in human terms, which is no small task. There are seven Greek words used throughout the New Testament that describe different aspects or manifestations of the omnipotent power of God. An understanding of these terms will help us to comprehend the transcending power and ability of the Holy Spirit to transform every life and situation that He touches, and to fulfill the highest purposes of God in the earth. Studying the power of God should inspire wonder and awe in our hearts and cause us to bow in worship before Him. How can we comprehend the greatness of the God who desires fellowship with man so earnestly that He uses all His divine power to redeem us and bring us into relationship with Himself? Such divine love is what the Holy Spirit came to reveal to us as He works to transform us into the image of Christ.

The Scriptures reveal many acts of the awesome power of God. We first glimpse His omnipotent power in the creation of the universe. The power of the Holy Spirit in Creation brought forth something out of nothing through the Word of God. The Scriptures teach us that mankind can recognize God simply by beholding the awesome wonders of His creation (Rom. 1:19–20). Another manifestation of the power of the Holy Spirit is in His military strength and might, the kind we would expect to see in an army. The hosts of heaven are endued with this kind of power. When Joshua was preparing to take the children of Israel into the Promised Land, God appeared to him as a mighty warrior. Joshua did not recognize Him at first and asked, "Art thou for us, or for our adversaries?" (Josh. 5:13). The reply came, "Nay; but as captain of the host of the LORD am I now come. And Joshua fell on his face to the earth, and did worship" (v. 14). This divine military power gave the Israelites victory over the giants of the land.

The resurrection power of the Holy Spirit is that power that raised Christ from the dead. Resurrection power is greater than the power of death. Christ conquered death, hell, and the grave through the resurrection power of the Holy Spirit. Paul wrote of this power, "But if the Spirit of him that raised up Jesus from the dead dwell in you, he that raised up Christ from the dead shall also quicken your mortal bodies by his Spirit that dwelleth in you" (Rom. 8:11). It is that resurrection power that gives us ultimate victory over death.

The Holy Spirit also is that dynamic force that equips a person for service. The Spirit makes a believer effective in destroying supernatural forces of darkness through miraculous and wonderful works. The power of the Holy Spirit also brings to man a moral strength that can elevate as well as calm an individual soul or a society that follows after godliness. The Holy Spirit is the power of Christ visibly operative in an assembled church that has Christ as its Head. This kingly power of God is discerning; it acts in divine knowledge upon the minds of men in manifold wisdom, revealing Jesus to those who believe. The power of the Holy Spirit moves in healing for the sick and in working of miracles. He is the divine Power of God who is able "to do exceeding abundantly above all that we ask or think, according to the power that worketh in us" (Eph. 3:20).

Having declared all that, we must still acknowledge our finite limitation in describing the omnipotent power of the living God. Do we really know Him? There are those who have attributed only one or two of these aspects of power to the Holy Spirit. Perhaps they think He came to give them the gift of tongues, or to bring deliverance from demonic oppression. Though these are aspects of His power, they do not comprehensively represent His Person. We dare not limit our understanding of His work to one or two manifestations of His power. If we do, what will happen when we discover we need Someone to exchange our sinful Adamic nature for a Christlike nature? Who will deliver us from anger, malice, and jealousy? Who will transform our minds to give us the mind of Christ? Who will take our moral weakness and give us strength to love God and serve Him? We need to know the Holy Spirit in all the omnipotent power of His Person. Then we must allow His divine power to work in and through us so His complete will and purpose can be accomplished.

1. Archē

The Greek word *archē* describes the divine power that can create something out of nothing. It is that power that brings forth something from itself as the source or beginning. We recognize in the root form of the word *archē* the English electrical term *arc* that defines a natural power source. That electrical arc that is the point of ignition for man's machinery gives us an accurate picture of this divine creative power of the Holy Spirit.

In Creation

God's creative power set the universe in motion with His Word. "In the beginning was the Word, and the Word was with God, and the Word was God.…All things were made by him; and without him was not any thing made that was made" (John 1:1, 3). When God created the world, He simply spoke it into existence through His divine power. "And the spirit of God moved upon the face of the waters. And God said, Let there be light: and there was light" (Gen. 1:2–3). It is this omnipotent power of creating a "beginning" that man's mind cannot comprehend, for we are incapable of creating in that sense.

The Scriptures teach us that "through faith we understand that the worlds were framed by the word of God, so that things which are seen were not made of things which do appear" (Heb. 11:3). Only by believing can we grasp the greatness of God's creative power. Again, concerning the beginning of Creation, we read, "And, Thou, Lord, in the beginning [*archē*] hast laid the foundation of the earth; and the heavens are the works of thine hands" (Heb. 1:10). As created beings, we are a result of this *archē* power of God that initiated life as we know it.

The Incarnation

The Incarnation of the Son of God is also an example of this creative power resident in the Holy Spirit. In the Scriptures, the angel told Mary that "the power of the Highest shall overshadow thee" and "the Holy Ghost shall come upon thee" (Luke 1:35). Both statements are synonymous expressions (Matt. 1:18–20; Isa. 7:14; Luke 1:35). One depicts the Divine source, and the other His holiness. The sinlessness of Jesus was not due to the sinlessness of His mother, but to the divine origin of His human nature, the Spirit of God (Heb. 10:5).[1] And "the Word became flesh, and dwelt among us" (John 1:14, NAS). The *archē* power of the Holy Spirit made possible the Incarnation of Christ—God becoming man.

New creation

Concerning the beginning of our Christian lives, John declares, "If that which ye have heard from the beginning [*archē*] shall remain in you, ye also shall continue in the Son, and in the Father" (1 John 2:24). The *archē* power of the Holy Spirit is like the switch that starts the ignition; it brings man into contact with God. The Spirit initiates a good work in us by His divine power, and then He continues to perfect that work in our lives. Peter declared that we are born again "not of corruptible seed, but of incorruptible, by the word of God, which liveth and abideth for ever" (1 Pet. 1:23). Christ literally comes to live within us, through His incorruptible life, when we are born again. The apostle Paul taught, "Therefore if any man be in Christ, he is a new creature: old things are passed away; behold, all things are become new" (2 Cor. 5:17). Accepting Jesus as our Savior ignites the *archē* power of God in our spirits, which creates eternal life. Because the creative power of God has come into the life of a believer, "Christ in you, the hope of glory" becomes a living reality (Col. 1:27).

In prayer

I believe the Holy Ghost wants us to live so we can touch the presence of God at all times. As we come to the place of prayer, we need this *archē* power to ignite faith in our hearts and bring our thoughts and desires into the presence of God. Every effective prayer has the divine power of God as its source. As we learn to yield to the Holy Spirit's power to inspire our prayer lives, we will know much more effectiveness in receiving answers to our prayers. The creative power of the spoken word on our lips, when energized by the power of the Holy Spirit, will bring supernatural results. It is through this kind of prayer that God accomplishes His will.

2. Exousia

Exousia, another Greek word translated into English as "power," particularly denotes the ability to decide and perform an action without hindrance. *Exousia* is the decisive authority of God. This word is usually used with *archē,* the power that sparks *exousia.* By connotation *exousia* reflects the power and the right to influence and enforce, the kind of right that government officials exercise. It depicts authority as well as divine ability to perform a task. Nothing happens even in this fallen world without the operation of e*xousia,* the divine authority of God.

When the scribes asked Jesus what right He had to forgive sins, Jesus replied, "Whether is it easier to say to the sick of the palsy, Thy sins be forgiven thee; or to say, Arise, and take up thy bed, and walk? But that ye may know that the Son of man hath power [*exousia*] on earth to forgive sins…" (Mark 2:9–10). The authority and jurisdiction to forgive was part of the power of God manifested in Jesus on earth. The scribes knew that God had the power to forgive sins. But, instead of concluding that Jesus was the Son of God because He demonstrated the power to forgive sins, they called Him a blasphemer. By denying the *exousia* power of God, they revealed a wicked heart of unbelief that could not enter the kingdom of God.

It is this decisive aspect of *exousia* power that enables us to enter the kingdom of God. "But as many as received him, to them gave he power to become the sons of God, even to them that believe on his name" (John 1:12). We cannot become sons of God without first receiving the power to do so. It is the power of the Holy Spirit that convicts men of sin (John 16:8) and causes them to confess Jesus as Lord (1 Cor. 12:3). The word *convict* means "cognitive process, for example, to reprove, refute, or convince." It also signifies a moral process beyond the mental activity, a moral conquest of our mind and our actions. The Holy Spirit endows the Christian life from beginning to end with moral character. We live the life exemplified by Christ through the empowering of the Spirit. Thus the Christian life is inherently and essentially supernatural. We are free to reject or accept this supernatural *exousia* power for our lives. If we reject it, then we cannot know God, for it is this power of His that gives us the ability to know Him. Everything we have we receive from God, who offers us His *exousia* so we may become His children.

After becoming children of God, we begin to realize our need for fellowship with other Christians. God ordained the existence of a body of believers known as the *Church* to reflect the life of Christ in the earth. "And he gave some, apostles; and some, prophets; and some, evangelists; and some, pastors and teachers; for the perfecting of the saints, for the work of the ministry, for the edifying of the body of Christ" (Eph. 4:11–12). As the Holy Spirit gives these ministries, He enables these people through divine *exousia* to lead others to grow in God. Paul declared to the Corinthians, "For though I should boast somewhat more of our authority [*exousia*], which the Lord hath given us for edification, and not for your destruction, I should not be ashamed" (2 Cor. 10:8). God gave Paul his authority and ability to edify the Church. Thank God for

His divine enabling that He gives to us to become a glorious Church, transformed into the image of His Son.

3. Ischus

Ischus expresses the boisterous, valiant, almighty force of divine power with its ability to penetrate opposition. Military force demonstrates this kind of power. We could call this the "bulldozer breath." The Book of Acts refers to the force of the preached Word of God as *ischus* power: "So mightily grew the word of God and prevailed" (Acts 19:20). It was this supernatural power of the preached Word that convinced thousands of people to turn to Christ for forgiveness of their sins. Later the apostle John declared, "I have written unto you, young men, because ye are strong [*ischus*], and the word of God abideth in you, and ye have overcome the wicked one" (1 John 2:14). The meaning of *power* in this text is "divine strength to conquer supernatural foes." Jesus admonished the disciples to ask for this mighty strength that they not be overthrown in the approaching disasters of the last time and that they be able to stand before the Son of Man (Luke 21:36). God's *ischus* power would deliver them and bring them to their goal.

4. Didōmi

The root meaning of the Greek word *didōmi* translates as "the power to give." Concerning God's giving Jesus to the world, this *didōmi* power reveals the realistic character of love as a gift, not just as a disposition. There is the power of action, not just of feeling, in love. God's love gave Jesus specific works to accomplish while on earth. It was the love of God reaching out to man that healed the sick, fed the hungry, and raised the dead. His love compelled Him to give life to those who asked for it and ultimately to lay down His own life so He might have many brethren.

Jesus declared, "All that the Father gives Me shall come to Me, and the one who comes to Me I will certainly not cast out" (John 6:37, NAS). It was neither Jesus' strength of personality nor monetary benefits that drew His disciples to Him. It was the supernatural power of God that gave men as disciples to Jesus. Even though many turned away when Jesus declared Himself to be the bread of life, there were still those who received the power of God to choose to follow Him.

When Jesus asked His disciples if they would turn away also, Peter declared, "Lord, to whom shall we go? You have words of eternal life" (John 6:68, NAS). They received the *didōmi* power of God that caused them to give their lives to following Jesus. Jesus prayed, "I manifested Thy name to the men whom Thou gavest Me out of the world; Thine they were, and Thou gavest them to Me, and they have kept Thy word" (John 17:6, NAS). Jesus clearly acknowledged here that it was the love of God that gave men the power to become disciples of Christ.

Jesus' death reveals the ultimate power of that "giving" love, which was willing and able to suffer the supreme sacrifice for the salvation of mankind. Jesus' death proves the boldness of conviction and courage, the determined power to win and to conquer that is inherent in godly love. Some have spoken of the love of God as "tough love," describing the fiber of determination and longing that characterizes His love. He will not be denied the object of His affections, despite those who deny Him. Still, His great love is pursuing man as the "Sheriff of the skies," desiring to arrest man's attention from his destructive course of sin and turn his feet toward everlasting life.

Among the Jews, *didōmi* power was the word often used to refer to the death of martyrs. Martyrs were those people who were forced to die a torturous death if they did not recant their faith in Christ. They possessed a supernatural power to lay down their lives for what they believed. It is this *didōmi* power of God that helps us to overcome our timidity and fears in the face of men and devils and to share boldly and courageously with others the life He has given us. Through the power of the Holy Spirit we will be compelled to give to others the life we have received from God.

5. Megaleiotēs

Megaleiotēs is the Greek word for power that refers to the magnificence and majesty of God as seen in the transfiguration of Christ. Peter recorded for us the majesty of that event:

> For we did not follow cleverly devised tales when we made known to you the power and coming of our Lord Jesus Christ, but we were eyewitnesses of His majesty. For when He received honor and glory from God the Father, such an utterance as this was made to Him by

> the Majestic Glory, "This is My beloved Son
> with whom I am well-pleased"—and we our-
> selves heard this utterance made from heaven
> when we were with Him on the holy mountain.
> —2 PETER 1:16–18, NAS

The majestic power of Christ cannot be fully compre-
hended by finite human minds. Peter said they were witnesses of His majesty and described that experience to
convince those believers of the reality of Christ's majestic
power. In another instance of *megaleiotēs* power, Jesus cast
out the devil that the disciples were unable to cast out. The
Scriptures describe the reaction of the crowd: "And they
were all amazed at the greatness [*megaleiotēs*] of God"
(Luke 9:43, NAS). *Megaleiotēs* power is that transcending
power of God that lifts humanity out of its impossible
plight and transforms impossible situations. It is a beautiful word picture that describes the kind of power used to
energize a freight elevator of a large industry. The freight
elevator is built to hold much more weight than elevators
used for transporting only people. Its cargo is too heavy
for the guest elevators. Also, it is usually hidden from the
eyes of the public. It is this "pulley power" of the Holy
Spirit that can lift a burden that would otherwise be
impossible to carry. The Holy Spirit Himself becomes our
"Burden Bearer." He pulls us out of sin, out of self, out of
our negative circumstances and grief, and He seats us in
heavenly places with Christ Jesus (Eph. 2:6).

Have you ever watched people go through severe trials
with peace and near serenity? They can have peace because

they have learned to know this transcending power of the Holy Spirit, the power that lifts them above their circumstances. They have learned to let Him carry the load too heavy for the human psyche. They find themselves seated in heavenly places in Christ Jesus, carried there by the power of the Holy Spirit. His power can transcend all human tragedy and lift us to a place of victorious living.

6. Energia

Energia is the important Greek word for power that refers to a divine energizing force that works effectually and powerfully. The Scriptures themselves possess this kind of divine power to save our souls. James taught us to "receive with meekness the engrafted word, which is able to save your souls" (James 1:21). Paul also wrote concerning the Scriptures: "For the word of God is quick, and powerful, and sharper than any two-edged sword, piercing even to the dividing asunder of soul and spirit, and of the joints and marrow, and is a discerner of the thoughts and intents of the heart" (Heb. 4:12). This verse describes the divine *energia* that cuts through the darkness of our souls as a laser beam of light cuts through flesh. The Word of God pierces our minds and emotions, revealing to us the deceptions and impure motives of our heart. Without the energizing power of the Holy Spirit coming in conviction to make the Word alive to our hearts, we could never be free from bondage to sin.

The Holy Spirit not only energizes our repentance, but He also gives us divine strength to share our faith with others. Paul prayed for Philemon and his friends that they would know this power of the Holy Spirit. He prayed for them, "that the communication of thy faith may become effectual by the acknowledging of every good thing which is in you in Christ Jesus" (Philem. 6). It is this energizing power of God "which worketh in you both to will and to do of his good pleasure" (Phil. 2:13).

This *energia* power is what I felt when God so gloriously healed me and granted me many more years to preach the Word of God. It is an exhilarating, invigorating, zealous power that rejoices in the conquering mood of the Holy Spirit as He quickens us and makes us alive to God. This divine energy causes us to live as effective lights in the darkness of this corrupt generation (Acts 2:40).

7. Kratos

Our final word, *kratos*, denotes the superior power of God to which the final victory belongs. In Peter's doxology, he writes, "To him be glory and dominion for ever and ever. Amen" (1 Pet. 5:11). This dominion is the ultimate triumph that belongs only to God. Paul prayed that the Church might be "strengthened with all might, according to his glorious power, unto all patience and longsuffering with joyfulness" (Col. 1:11). Only as this divine *kratos* power of the Holy Spirit strengthens us supernaturally can we triumph ultimately over evil.

Jude declares, "To the only wise God our Saviour, be glory and majesty, dominion and power, both now and ever. Amen" (Jude 25). He acknowledges God as the eternal

Victor over all the power of evil. John the Revelator sums up the eternal significance of this power in the sacrifice of Christ. He wrote:

> And every creature which is in heaven, and on the earth, and under the earth, and such as are in the sea, and all that are in them, heard I saying, Blessing, and honour, and glory, and power, be unto him that sitteth upon the throne, and unto the Lamb for ever and ever.
> —REVELATION 5:13

Eternal dominion belongs to God alone, who has triumphed by His great power. Our appropriation of this power ensures our ultimate victory in our individual lives and in the Church corporately.

Summary

This brief consideration of the sevenfold power of the Holy Spirit reveals an infinite, all-encompassing, eternal power that is competent to meet every conceivable need of mankind. The Holy Spirit fulfills God's purpose to redeem mankind from sin. However, eternal purpose is not just to take us to heaven, but to make it possible for us to live victoriously here on earth. God's ultimate goal will be realized in a glorious Church without spot or wrinkle. As believers who learn to yield to the Holy Spirit and who come into right relationship with Him, we discover the omnipotent power that He offers. He changes us from the image of the fallen Adam into that of the Last Adam, Jesus

Christ. He forms in us the character of God—God's own nature—as we continue to exercise our free volition and choose His life.

Why do we not see His power displayed in a greater way in the Church? I believe the answer to that indicting question is we have not made ourselves available to Him. We have not yielded completely to Him, to where His life-giving power can flow through us to meet our personal needs as well as the needs of others. Through His great power He is able, but we don't make ourselves available to Him. We depend on our own ability to face our life circumstances instead of cultivating a dependence on the power of the Holy Spirit.

God demonstrated His power when He took twelve men, filled them with the Holy Ghost, and used them to turn the world upside down—without the help of the media or any modern evangelistic method. The power of the Holy Spirit consumed these men and filled them with His purpose to win the world for Christ. They yielded to the supernatural power of the Holy Spirit as a prerequisite for living a supernatural life in Christ. So as we come into right relationship with the Holy Spirit, the same zeal that motivated those first apostles will consume us as well. Then we can truly experience the love of the God whose great desire to save mankind caused Him to give His life for them. Signs and wonders will again follow those who believe, as we expect to receive the supernatural power of the Holy Spirit for all of life's situations. Then we will also turn our world upside down to the glory of Christ and the building of His kingdom.

Seven Moods of the Holy Spirit, Part I

Divine Purposes Expressed

If we think of the term *mood* in a common human sense, we may misunderstand the entire concept of the moods of the Holy Spirit. We speak of people having good moods and bad moods. We often characterize people's behavior by saying they are moody. That is not a very positive way to describe people. It usually means they are immature and temperamental, given to depression. However, this negative connotation of moodiness is not inherent to the word's definition. A mood can be defined simply as a conscious state of mind or predominant emotion. We can expect the Holy Spirit, as a divine Person, to function in a conscious state of mind and to express emotion in righteousness. It is only our unredeemed human psyches that create "bad" moods that are sinful.

When we discuss the moods of the Holy Spirit, we are describing a frame of mind He uses to express Himself to reveal His divine purpose for a particular situation. The Holy Spirit responds differently to different kinds of situations, though in each situation His ultimate purpose is to reveal Jesus and to fulfill the Father's eternal plan for mankind. For example, at times He will come in a convicting mood to convince men of sin. He expresses a compassionate mood when He comes as the Comforter to someone who is suffering grief.

As we describe the work of the Holy Spirit, we want to keep in mind that His moods often are expressed through human vessels. We are temples of the Holy Spirit, forming the body of Christ in the earth (1 Cor. 3:16). The Holy Spirit does much of His work through us. So it is important for us to recognize the different moods of the Holy Spirit. Only then can we understand what He is doing and why He is expressing Himself through us in those ways. Only then can we cooperate with Him in fulfilling His purposes for His Church. Yet no matter what mood He is revealing through a human vessel at a given time, His purpose never is to exalt or call attention to that person. Exalting our fleshly nature does not promote His ultimate goal of revealing Jesus.

Unfortunately, many things that have been done in the name of the Holy Spirit have resulted in exalting a personality. The Holy Spirit's work is to exalt Jesus, not people. When human personality prevails in a situation above the exaltation of Jesus, it is out of order.

The Scriptures teach that Jesus made Himself of no reputation (Phil. 2:7). The Holy Spirit also reflects this same self-effacing spirit of humility that reveals His beautiful consecration and love for the Father. He humbled Himself in Jesus so the Father might be glorified. The Holy Spirit does not make a reputation for Himself or for our flesh. Everything we receive from the Holy Spirit should result in others seeing Jesus in us. If we receive healing for our bodies or revelation from the Word, we should not allow ourselves to rejoice as much in those gifts as we do in the Giver of those gifts. As humility characterizes the Godhead, so every mood of the Holy Spirit expresses that humility, even through human vessels. As we walk with the Holy Spirit as a Person, we will become sensitive to His moods as He expresses the humility of Christ in our lives.

Convicting Mood

Conviction may be defined as an act of pleading, beseeching, or reproving. The Holy Spirit comes to us in this frame of mind to make us God conscious and aware of our sinful nature and sinful acts. Jesus told His disciples that He would send the Counselor to them. He said, "When he comes, he will convict the world of guilt in regard to sin and righteousness and judgment" (John 16:8, NIV). Jesus was describing the convicting mood of the Holy Spirit.

Billy Graham has stated that one key to his ministry is

the careful attention he gives to the altar calls. The ministry team allows no moving or leaving during that time, for that is the time the Holy Spirit comes in conviction to hearts that have heard the preached Word of God. In those moments, if people respond to the pleading of the Holy Spirit, they can come to true salvation of their souls and be born again to an eternal relationship with God. The Holy Spirit comes gently but irresistibly in His love to show people their guilt before a holy God and to point them to the Savior who can deliver them from their sin.

Conviction or condemnation?

Conviction from the Holy Spirit must not be confused with thoughts and feelings of condemnation. Conviction is constructive and full of hope. The Holy Spirit comes in convicting power to make us sorry for our sin and to bring us to repentance. When the Holy Spirit convicts us, He shows us exactly what sin we need to repent of. When we acknowledge our sin, we find relief in repenting of it and experience joy in accepting forgiveness. The voice of condemnation, on the contrary, is an accusing voice that speaks of failure and defeat. If we receive a mental suggestion of vague accusation that takes us into depression and despair, we have listened to the condemning voice of the enemy. These tormenting thoughts tell us such things as, "You are no good, and you will never be any different. You're so bad God is mad at you. He cannot or will not forgive you." Those accusations are the enemy's work of condemnation.

God never intended for us to feel condemnation. Jesus

declared, "For God sent not his Son into the world to condemn the world; but that the world through him might be saved" (John 3:17). The Holy Spirit came as a Helper, a *Paraclete*, a Counselor, and a Teacher. His convicting work will result in our coming closer to Christ, not in our wallowing in despair. Without the convicting power of the Holy Spirit we would be helplessly lost in our sin. He is faithful to shine His light on areas of darkness in our lives so we can be cleansed from all unrighteousness.

Our correct response to conviction will produce true repentance in our lives. True repentance is not just an expression of sorrow for what we have done; it is a complete turning away from the revealed sin. Repentance should become a way of life for us, not a one-time expression of confessed guilt before receiving salvation. As we behold the holiness of God and see ourselves as God sees us, each new revelation brings fresh conviction that produces repentance. Our joy becomes fuller each time we are set free from an area of bondage to sin. Although the revelation of our sin may bring pain, the deliverance from its power results in the kingdom of God coming to us in righteousness, peace, and joy in the Holy Ghost (Rom. 14:17). We are made whole as we learn to yield to the convicting mood of the Holy Spirit.

Counseling Mood

The counseling mood of the Holy Spirit reveals the divine Teacher. I believe that the greatest work of the Holy Spirit is teaching, for without the teaching mood He could not do any of His other work. Every new revelation and realm of light we discover in God results from the work of the Holy Spirit, who came to teach us and guide us into all truth (John 14:26; 16:13). Whatever mood the Holy Spirit is manifesting, His objective is to teach us the will of God. He teaches about sin and convicts us. He teaches us how to pray. He teaches us about eternity. He comes to reveal Jesus to us. He opens dimensions of life to us so we can see who we are in the sight of God, what we need at the moment, and where we are going in the future.

The best teacher is the one who gets involved with the student in the subject he is teaching. A true teacher doesn't talk down to students but takes a posture alongside them. Nicodemus and others called Jesus "a teacher come from God" (John 3:2). The two disciples walking on the road to Emmaus exclaimed, "Did not our heart burn within us, while he talked with us by the way, and while he opened to us the scriptures?" (Luke 24:32). Jesus taught them while they were on the way. In this same manner, the Holy Spirit has come to be our Teacher to reveal Jesus to us so we can walk in a personal relationship with God and then share that relationship with others. The Holy Spirit is the ultimate Teacher who gets involved with us and helps us learn by walking beside us in our life situations.

However, because of the fall of man, sin has blinded us to eternal truths. We cannot receive truth from God unless the Holy Spirit reveals it to us. God desires so much for us to know Him that He uses all kinds of language techniques in the Scriptures to give us a picture of Himself. He wrote to us in types, shadows, allegories, metaphors, parables, parabolic expressions, similes, and sometimes hyperbole to reach us with His heavenly message. Then the Holy Spirit takes the written Word and makes it alive inside us. John wrote, "And the Word was made flesh, and dwelt among us" (John 1:14). He understood that God's Word is not law but a Person. The Holy Spirit unveils the Person of Jesus within our lives, and the Word is made flesh within us as God forms His character and nature in us. That is why I think the greatest role of the Holy Spirit is as a Teacher who reveals Jesus to us so He might be unveiled in us.

Adam and his wife were forbidden to eat of the tree of the knowledge of good and evil lest they die (Gen. 2:17). When they chose to eat of that tree, they died to their relationship with God. Their disobedience produced in them a carnal mind that was hostile to God (Rom. 8). The world's philosophies of humanism, atheism, skepticism, communism, New Age, and any other self-centered rationale have their roots in this first disobedience. Humanistic philosophy reflects this alienation from God by placing man at the center of his personal universe, independent from God. That independence, which is the root of all sin, resulted in God's removing man from the garden so he would not have access to the tree of life, which was there as well. If they had eaten of the tree of life in their sinful state, they would have lived forever in that condition, dead to God.

When man refused to be dependent upon God, he lost

the mind of God, which is the source of all truth. That is when the "veil of flesh" first divided the inner chamber of man, separating the soul of man from his spirit. Man's spirit was intended to be "the way" to the Father's house. When Jesus came declaring, "I am the way, the truth, and the life" (John 14:6), He gave hope to all mankind for their reconciliation to God. Man could have relationship with God through this new and living way, through the blood of Jesus (Heb. 10:19–20). Everyone who receives Christ can experience truth and life as God intended it. Unless the Spirit of Truth reveals the "Tree of Life" to us and replants it in the garden of our hearts through the new birth, we will not have the abundant life God ordained.

The Holy Spirit came to teach us so we would not be ignorant of life. Paul spoke of this ignorance when writing to the Ephesian church. He explained how the carnal mind works and then contrasted it with the mind that is taught of Christ:

> This I say therefore, and testify in the Lord, that ye henceforth walk not as other Gentiles walk, in the vanity of their mind, having the understanding darkened, being alienated from the life of God through the ignorance that is in them, because of the blindness of their heart: who being past feeling have given themselves over unto lasciviousness, to work all uncleanness with greediness. But ye have not so learned Christ; if so be that ye have heard him, and have been taught by him, as the truth is in

> Jesus: that ye put off concerning the former conversation the old man, which is corrupt according to the deceitful lusts; and be renewed in the spirit of your mind; and that ye put on the new man, which after God is created in righteousness and true holiness.
>
> —Ephesians 4:17–24

Paul expected the believers to be different from Gentiles, from people without Christ, in their thinking and in their speech. The Holy Spirit comes as a Teacher to give us divine counsel and to restore truth to our minds so we can know the abundant life that Jesus promised us. As we cooperate with Him and put off our former ungodly thinking and conversation, allowing our carnal minds to be transformed, we begin to think the thoughts God intended us to think. Thus our divine Counselor teaches us to live a life of righteousness and true holiness.

Compassion

> Oh that my head were waters, and mine eyes a fountain of tears, that I might weep day and night for the slain of the daughter of my people!
>
> —Jeremiah 9:1

This cry of Jeremiah reflects the compassionate mood of the Holy Spirit that can be called the weeping or tearful mood. It expresses God's tender caring for mankind.

Natural man cannot feel godly compassion. He may feel pity or sympathetic concern, but human emotions without God do not express true compassion.

True compassion is revealed only in the nature of God. It is suffering with another, commiserating with his distress, and desiring to show mercy to him. It is revealed in human hearts through a work of the Holy Spirit, when He gives us that godly ability to weep with those who weep (Rom. 12:15). Compassion is a mixed passion, one compounded of love and sorrow. Being compassionate means having a heart that is tender and easily moved by the distresses, sufferings, wants, and infirmities of others. Jesus wept over the city of Jerusalem because the Jews missed the day of their visitation (Luke 19:41–44). He was not offended that the Jews did not receive Him, but grieved. He had compassion on their ignorance and hardness of heart that kept them in darkness. He felt deeply their distress, and He desired to alleviate it.

When the Holy Spirit within us causes us to feel His compassion for a person, we weep with His brokenness and love. Paul instructed the Ephesians, "And be ye kind one to another, tenderhearted, forgiving one another, even as God for Christ's sake hath forgiven you" (Eph. 4:32). The more we walk in the Spirit, the more tenderhearted we will be. We will feel the same burdens operating in and through us that Christ feels when He looks on a sinful world. We will suffer the pain of love that is true compassion for lost people bound by sin. When we do, we experience the love and compassion of Christ flowing through us to help others who are in distress.

Cleansing Mood

When Jesus cleansed the temple in Jerusalem, He made a whip of small cords and drove out the moneychangers. "And his disciples remembered that it was written, The zeal of thine house hath eaten me up" (John 2:17). This zeal of our Lord was divine indignation at the defilement of the temple that God had intended to be a house of prayer, of power, of purpose, and of purity. When the Holy Spirit comes to cleanse our own temples, His zeal against sin causes Him deep distress. Paul declared, "Know ye not that ye are the temple of God, and that the Spirit of God dwelleth in you?" (1 Cor. 3:16). The Spirit of God, who is the essence of the holiness of God, comes to our hearts to cleanse us of all unholiness so He may dwell in peace in our temples. That does not mean He would not come to us in our imperfect, sinful state. But after He comes, He patiently shines His light on one area of unrighteousness after another until He has fulfilled His divine purpose of cleansing our temples and making us holy.

This cleansing mood is the censoring, holy cry of the inner man. It is the Spirit of God and the spirit of man crying out in union against what is immoral, sinful, unjust, and destructive to God's kingdom and to the body, soul, and spirit of man. When the Holy Spirit comes to cleanse His temples, He may seem angry and harsh to us. We may feel the scourge of cords driving out the wicked thing that is defiling our lives. Yet, if we understand correctly, we will be grateful that divine love is walking in our temples to deliver us from sin for His purposes. His anger is against the sin that threatens to destroy us. As we agree with Him and "confess our sins, he is faithful and just to forgive us our sins, and to cleanse us from all unrighteousness" (1 John 1:9). We need to yield to the cleansing mood of the Holy Spirit so we can be changed into the image of Christ.

Commanding Mood

When Jesus rebuked the waves and winds and demanded that they be calm when the storm threatened the disciples' lives, He revealed the commanding mood of the Holy Spirit. He stood in that small boat and cried, "Peace, be still" (Mark 4:39). Using the vernacular of today, He might have said, "Lie down, devil, and shut up!" Then the winds obeyed Jesus, to the disciples' astonishment. They did not yet understand the supernatural power of the Holy Spirit working through Him.

Paul, who was only a prisoner on a ship going to Italy, became commander of that ship by the power of the Holy Spirit during a crisis. When a violent storm at sea threatened the ship and the lives of all on board, and when the crew was ready to jump overboard, Paul began to command the situation by the authority of the Holy Spirit. He declared to those ungodly men that there would be no loss of life, although they would lose the ship. He said, "For this very night an angel of the God to whom I belong and whom I serve stood before me" (Acts 27:23, NAS). From that angel Paul received not only divine instructions for the situation but also the power to carry them out. Thus his life and the lives of all those on the ship were spared as they obeyed God's servant. It was the supernatural power of the Holy Spirit that commanded that situation. Paul was simply the human vessel used to do the will of God in that moment.

We seem to enjoy the commanding mood of the Holy Spirit more than the others and desire to see it manifested among us. We love to say to the enemy, "We command you to…" There are occasions when that is the proper response to the moving of the Holy Spirit. However, we need to remember that, as with all the moods of the Holy Spirit, His commanding mood is motivated by love. Because of man's inherent desire to rule, we need to be careful not to confuse natural "boldness" with the commanding mood of the Holy Spirit. Bossiness is not motivated by love. A person with a proud, commanding spirit is usually a person who is very insecure and desires to control others. Anyone who does not display a broken spirit and who is not teachable may simply be displaying a carnal desire to rule when commanding a situation. We can be thankful for the true commanding mood of the Holy Spirit that has authority and power to change any situation for God's glory.

Conquering Mood

When the Holy Spirit expresses Himself in the conquering mood, He is joyful, triumphant, and victorious. "For this purpose the Son of God was manifested, that he might destroy the works of the devil" (1 John 3:8). The original meaning of the Greek word used here for "destroy" is *luo*. It means that Jesus came to outdo, undo, and overdo everything the devil ever did. Truly understanding Jesus' ultimate triumph over evil makes us shout "Hallelujah!" When a person or a church realizes that kind of victory, the Holy Spirit is ready to rejoice as the conquering armies in Bible history did when they returned home with the spoils. In those days the whole city would turn out and line the streets to praise the soldiers as they marched home in triumph over their enemies.

After the Holy Spirit convicts us of sin and cleanses our temples through our repentance, we sense this triumph and joy of God's presence in our lives. In those times we cannot help but rejoice, praise, and shout about the goodness of God. He has conquered the sin that was trying to destroy us, and we are free to enjoy His blessings in our lives. When a person has sought for God and found Him, the divine Conqueror comes to bring rejoicing and to express His triumph over the devil's attempt to destroy that life. Exalting Jesus in praise expresses the conquering mood of the Holy Spirit. In this place of rejoicing, dancing, and shouting, we are aware that principalities and powers previously standing against us in the heavenlies have been brought down.

When David came against Goliath, he declared, "But I come to thee in the name of the LORD of hosts" (1 Sam. 17:45). His confidence was in the Lord, who was the conqueror of this giant and all the others who dared to defy God. I like to describe this conquering, joyful, and triumphant mood as the jubilation we feel when, through the power of the Holy Spirit, we have conquered every demon in sight! We have cut off Goliath's head and are standing on the top of the highest hill, rattling our other four smooth stones (1 Sam. 17:40), looking around to see if there are any more giants to be conquered. Someone has suggested that the other four rocks were for Goliath's four brothers. Surely the Lord has equipped us with five stones to fight the enemy. He has given us His name, His Word, His blood, His Spirit, and His faith. These stones, when exercised in the "sling" of praise, make us more than conquerors.

This same kind of jubilation accompanied the victory in another Old Testament crisis—when Haman as well as his sons were hung on the scaffold erected for Mordecai (Esther 9:25). In still another battle, when King Jehoshaphat faced a formidable enemy, he sent the singers and praisers ahead of the army, that they "should praise the beauty of holiness" (2 Chron. 20:21). Then God sent ambushments against the enemies, and these enemies proceeded to destroy themselves. Jehoshaphat's army didn't have to fight at all. They simply went and collected the spoils from the slain armies. Likewise the Holy Spirit is the mighty conqueror of the enemies who are too strong for us, and He will cause us to rejoice in triumphant victory when we see them defeated.

Summary

We have described six of the seven moods through which the Holy Spirit expresses His purposes. As we walk in the

Spirit, we learn to recognize His various moods when He expresses them in our individual lives and in the corporate expression of the Church. We must learn to yield to the Spirit of God within us, to agree with His purpose for the moment, and allow Him to weep or rejoice through us. We must accept His cleansing and listen to His commands. As we do, He will reveal Jesus to us, and He will lead and guide us into all truth. He will bring us into deep communion with the Father as we allow our personal relationship with God to become more intimate by cultivating a life of prayer.

The seventh mood of the Holy Spirit, which is the subject of the last chapter, is His communion mood. Communion between God and man has always been the ultimate goal of God's love. Yet we can scarcely begin to comprehend the love of God until we have first learned to commune with Him. The epitome of our relationship with the Holy Spirit is realized in learning to yield to His communion mood.

6

Seven Moods of the Holy Spirit, Part II

God's Desire for Mankind Realized

G od's ultimate desire for mankind is to commune with him so He can reveal His great love for him and communicate His will to him. He is able to do that through the communion mood of the Holy Spirit. The Holy Spirit expresses His communion mood through the multifaceted realms of prayer. We learned in an earlier chapter that the Holy Spirit comes to establish communion between our spirits and God, who is Spirit, as He works through the office of supplication.

Although the prayer mood of the Holy Spirit is integrally related with His office of prayer, we would miss much revelation of God's deep desire to commune with man if we did not study them separately. We can expect these two truths, the office of prayer and the mood of prayer, to overlap and intertwine, yet the revelation of each needs to be grasped in its singularity. Then comparing the Holy Spirit's work in the office of supplication with His communion mood will give us a more complete perspective of this many-faceted diamond of prayer.

Too often we think of prayer as simply our talking with God. We don't realize that God the Father, God the Son, and God the Holy Spirit want to talk to us in prayer. True prayer is two-way communication with God. In the broader meaning of the word, *communion* encompasses seven different aspects of prayer that the Holy Spirit uses to teach us to communicate with God. When we look at communion in its deepest meaning, however, we will understand that it is the most intimate of all realms of prayer. It is that relationship ordained of God to completely satisfy our hearts as well as His own. Every form of prayer has its necessary function and must be properly cultivated in the life of the believer; thus we need to understand the Holy Spirit's desire for each aspect of prayer.

Petition

We are all so familiar with the prayer of petition that we do not need to discuss it in detail. This is the kind of prayer that asks for what we and others need. The Scriptures are clear that we are to ask God for what we need. Paul taught us to make our requests known unto God with thanksgiving (Phil. 4:6). James wrote that we have not because we ask not or because we ask amiss (James 4:2–3). Jesus taught us to ask in His name and the Father would give us what we asked (John 16:23–24). Although the Scriptures clearly teach that we must bring our requests for things we need to God, we must be careful to watch our motivation for asking. It is easy to be selfish when we petition God, since the conversation in this kind of prayer is usually one-sided and self-centered. We need to be sure we are in agreement with the Holy Spirit in what we are asking and that our requests are promoting the kingdom of God and His will and purpose for our lives or for the lives of those people whom we are petitioning God for.

Thanksgiving

"It is a good thing to give thanks unto the Lord" (Ps. 92:1). The prayer of thanksgiving means to offer thanks to God from a grateful heart for what He has done. The psalmist taught us that thanksgiving is the proper way to enter the presence of God: "Enter into his gates with thanksgiving, and into his courts with praise: be thankful unto him, and bless his name" (Ps. 100:4). Our thanksgiving is to be a genuine thankfulness to the Lord for what He has done for us: for His mercy, His grace, His longsuffering, and His goodness to us. Listen to Paul's instructions: "In everything give thanks; for this is God's will for you in Christ Jesus" (1 Thess. 5:18, NAS). This command immediately follows his instruction to "pray without ceasing" (v. 17). Clearly, our attitude in prayer is to be one of thanksgiving.

If we have a thankful spirit, we will be thankful to other people and will express our gratitude freely. It is impossible to yield our minds to a critical spirit while we are enjoying a thankful heart. That should be reason enough for us to cultivate the attitude of thankfulness. According to the Scriptures, unthankfulness (ingratitude) will be a characteristic of people who live in the last days (2 Tim. 3:1–2). Paul taught the Ephesians that Christians should be "always giving thanks for all things in the name of our Lord Jesus Christ to God, even the Father" (Eph. 5:20, NAS). We need to cultivate expressing a spirit of gratitude as a way of life and offer prayers of thanksgiving continually to our God.

Supplication

As an aspect of the communion mood of the Holy Spirit, supplication applies specifically to the humble and earnest cry that comes from the deep desire of the spirit and soul. David cried out to the Lord, "Hear the voice of my supplications, when I cry unto thee" (Ps. 28:2). The Holy Spirit gives us these deep cries and yearnings for the will of God to be fulfilled in our lives and in the lives of others.

This was the testimony of the early church in the Book of Acts: "These all continued with one accord in prayer and supplication" (Acts 1:14). A study of the early church reveals the impact that earnest prayer had upon impossible situations; it brought supernatural intervention. Peter was delivered from prison by an angel on one occasion as the Church prayed (Acts 12). On another occasion the whole place where they were praying was shaken, and they were empowered to speak boldly amid the threatenings against them (Acts 4:31). God answered their fervent cries in their time of need.

To Timothy, Paul wrote, "I exhort therefore, that, first of all, supplications, prayers, intercessions, and giving of thanks, be made for all men; for kings, and for all that are in authority; that we may lead a quiet and peaceable life in all godliness and honesty" (1 Tim. 2:1–2). This command to pray for our leaders means more than a perfunctory "God bless you" that we might pray when we celebrate our national Independence Day. The Holy Spirit energizes us with heartfelt desires for the will of God to be done in the earth. God hears the cry of our supplications as we follow the scriptural admonition to pray earnestly. As individual believers who together form the Church, we need to evaluate the intensity of our prayer life. If we sense a lack of desire, we can ask the Holy Spirit to come and fill us with His deep cries of supplication.

Intercession

This is the prayer of standing in the gap for someone else. We notice that all three members of the Godhead intercede for and through us to fulfill the eternal plan and purpose of God for our lives, which is to be transformed into His image. Jesus ever lives to make intercession for us

(Heb. 7:25), and the Holy Spirit makes intercession for the saints according to the will of the Father (Rom. 8:26–27). Intercession is not a special ministry for only a few. Everyone who walks with the Holy Spirit knows intercession as He burdens their hearts for the needs of others. Many lives and churches have been snatched from the burning fire by the prayers of faithful intercessors.

Moses, the great intercessor, pleaded more than once for God to not destroy the rebellious nation of Israel as they wandered in the wilderness, murmuring and complaining. In that same way, God gives us burdens to pray for those around us. He trusts us to carry a burden of intercession for a life that would otherwise be destroyed. As we learn to yield to the Holy Spirit in intercession, we begin to pray until we see His wonderful answer in that life or situation.

Praise

We will look at praise and worship as two different ways of expressing our love to God. In praise we turn our eyes to God and away from ourselves. If we enter His gates with thanksgiving, we can go on into His courts with praise when we magnify Him for His greatness and His goodness (Ps. 100:4). In this context, praise means to make a show in raving about Him, to the point of being clamorously foolish. We praise Him for who He is and for His mighty acts toward the sons of men. We exalt Him as we recognize His love and power. Through praise we honor and give credit and homage to our Lord.

Worship

We do not define worship as a general term for coming to church or for singing praises. True worship occurs when our spirits have experienced a divine encounter with the living God. The Hebrew word for worship, *shachah*, can be translated as "bow down, crouch, do reverence, prostrate, and beseech humbly." The Greek word for worship most used in the New Testament is *proskuneo*. It means "to kiss toward." In worship the believer expresses the affection and deep devotion of his heart in the presence of God. The comprehensive meaning of worship, then, is to respect, esteem, love, admire, and reverence God. In its deepest sense, worship is a heart's response to the manifest presence of God.

Praise and worship contrasted

What is the difference between praise and worship? Although these terms are used interchangeably by some, we can see from our definitions that there is a significant difference we need to understand. The purpose of *praise* is to bring us into God's presence. *Worship* is our heart's response to Him when we come into a conscious realization of His presence. Praise and thanksgiving exalt God for what He has done. Worship is our love response to who He is; it is an inevitable response of the loving heart in the presence of God. When, for example, the curtain of heaven is drawn back and we get a glimpse of what is happening in the presence of God, we read, "And the four and twenty elders fell down and worshipped" (Rev. 5:14). God's manifest presence evokes such awe and reverence that often we cannot speak, but must prostrate ourselves before Him in worship. So we express our deepest love and adoration to the Lord in the place of worship.

God is seeking a people who will worship Him "in spirit and in truth" (John 4:23). When Isaiah was in the presence of God, he saw the truth about himself and cried, "Woe is me" (Isa. 6:5). In the place of worship we not only see God but also our sinfulness in comparison to a holy God. Then we worship Him by repenting and pouring out our wills and desires at His feet in prayer, asking for His will to be done. In return, we receive His life-giving, eternal purposes for us. In worship we have a vital key to personal change. True worship presupposes a life of submission to the Lordship of Christ. It expresses our comprehensive devotion to God out of love for Him and out of all-consuming passion to please Him in all.

Profitable values of praise and worship

Many of us learned to praise and worship before we knew the implications of where God was leading us. Have you ever asked the question, "What does worship do for me?" Worshiping Him is ordained by God as the highest purpose for mankind. As we learn to walk in that purpose, however, what can we expect as the results in our lives?

The presence of God is manifested. First we can expect praise and worship to bring the manifest presence of God into our midst. As we saw earlier, the Bible teaches the omnipresence of God (meaning God is everywhere). It teaches the abiding presence of God for believers (John 15). It reveals God's manifest presence every time He moves supernaturally in behalf of His people. God desires to manifest His presence to our lives and in our churches. True worship brings His manifest presence to His people.

Right relationship is achieved. Worship brings us into right relationship with Christ. "One thing have I desired of the Lord, that will I seek after; that I may dwell in the house of the Lord all the days of my life, to behold the beauty of the Lord, and to inquire in his temple" (Ps. 27:4). Why do you suppose God said through Samuel to Saul, "The Lord hath sought him a man after his own heart" (1 Sam. 13:14)? David had learned that the greatest satisfaction man can experience is to worship God.

That is why we were created in the beginning: to have fellowship with our heavenly Father. Fellowship is that free communication of loving hearts one to another. David did not ask for either material or temporal things; his desire was for fellowship and communion with the Lord. Fellowship is established through our prayer life. What is our own fellowship (prayer life) like? David prayed, "Let my prayer be set forth before thee as incense; and the lifting up of my hands as the evening sacrifice" (Ps. 141:2). In God's plan, prayer fellowship is the link to a higher realm of worship.

Divine love is received. When we experience God's manifest presence of divine love, He gives us divine ability to love one another genuinely. Jesus said, "A new commandment I give unto you, That ye love one another" (John 13:34). If we are honest with God and with ourselves, we will admit that this command has been extremely difficult to obey. The natural man does not love the unlovely. We love those who are loving, who are attentive to us, and perhaps those who serve us. But what is our reaction to even a Christian brother who is irritating, insulting, or in some way obnoxious?

At our conversion we received a measure of divine love for one another, and that love deepens when we receive the baptism of the Holy Spirit. Yet often our own prejudices, opinions, and natural feelings hinder the expression of His love through us to others. If our ideas are challenged, for example, or our opinions crossed or our plan is not honored, how do we react? Are we tolerant and understanding of others' views?

Or are we like the disciples whom Jesus rebuked when He said, "Ye know not what manner of spirit ye are of" (Luke 9:55)? That is where guile and pretense have their entrance. We know that love is the scriptural pattern and requirement, so we strive to act in a loving way. But many times we only play the part without experiencing the reality of love in our hearts.

Worship changes the picture. As we worship God with extravagant love and complete submission, He changes our perspective! We perceive the "Christ" in each other. Although faults and imperfections are still there, love forgives and overlooks them. When our vision is horizontally (earthly) inclined, we see only trouble and heartache. But if we lift our eyes vertically, looking to Jesus, we see people as God sees them. Then we can love them as He does. Worship gives us God's perspective of life.

A throne is in our midst. The Scriptures teach that God is enthroned on our praises (Ps. 22:3). We enthrone Him as we worship at His footstool. As we worship corporately around His throne, He unites our hearts and establishes His harmony in the Church. In a prophetic vision the prophet Joel described that unity: "And they shall march every one on his ways, and they shall not break their ranks: neither shall one thrust another; they shall walk every one in his path" (Joel 2:7–8). Joel was describing the unity the Church would know as a military force, marching in formation. He saw prophetically the beauty of a great host of people in total harmony. To be a part of that army requires daily discipline and training, both individually and corporately. Each soldier must commit himself unreservedly to the one who gives the commands. The life of the whole depends on the total cooperation of each individual. The Church today is vigorously striving for unity but often finding none. True unity will come only when the Church experiences spiritual worship.

The apostle Paul gave us a picture of unity when he described the Church as a body: "Now ye are the body of Christ, and members in particular" (1 Cor. 12:27). Each member surrenders his privilege of individual recognition and decisions to become a living, vital "supply joint" that provides increase and mobility to the body of Christ, the Church. We know there is power in unity, and we want to walk in it. But it seems that when we get one member in his place, another will break rank. Jealously, envy, bitterness, and strife infiltrate the ranks no matter how valiantly we labor. The wisdom of the hour is to find out which way God is moving and to get into step with Him. Worship in the presence of God melts our hearts and brings us to repentance for wrong attitudes that cause disunity.

Worship places us on the offensive. One outward form of praise involves the lifting up the hands. The psalmist cried, "Lift up your hands in the sanctuary, and bless the LORD" (Ps. 134:2). Raising our hands can be a sign of surrender and can testify to the resurrection power of Christ. It can represent an aspect of warfare as well. The psalmist acknowledged that the Lord was with his hands in battle when he wrote, "Blessed be the LORD my strength, which teacheth my hands to war, and my fingers to fight" (Ps. 144:1). Warfare is a part of life for every Christian who expects to be victorious over his enemies.

David understood that praise was an effective weapon against his enemies. He wrote, "Out of the mouth of babes and sucklings hast thou ordained strength because of thine enemies" (Ps. 8:2). When Jesus quoted the psalmist, He substituted the word *praise* for the word *strength*: "Out of the mouth of babes and sucklings thou hast perfected praise" (Matt. 21:16). Praise is a spiritual strength against our enemies when we learn to truly worship the Lord in spirit and truth. What does this praise do? It stills the avenger and puts the enemy to flight. That is the reason Satan hates worship; it puts him to flight. David instructed the saints to be joyful and to "let the high praises of God be in their mouth, and a two-edged sword in their hand" (Ps. 149:6). In this way we are to defeat all our enemies. We assume our offensive position

through worship and actually make war in high places.
Paul understood this when he wrote:

> For the weapons of our warfare are not carnal,
> but mighty through God to the pulling down
> of strong holds; casting down imaginations,
> and every high thing that exalteth itself
> against the knowledge of God, and bringing
> into captivity every thought to the obedience
> of Christ.
> —2 CORINTHIANS 10:4–5

One of Satan's most effective maneuvers is to attack our thought life and cause us to imagine all sorts of unrealities. How often have you been tormented by feelings of unworthiness, guilt, or just vague uneasiness concerning your relationship with God? It would be wonderful to just "take our minds out of gear" so nothing could affect us. Since that is impossible, we either fill our minds with godly thoughts or the enemy invades us with lying vanities. Praising God establishes a proper perspective and becomes a spiritual weapon that pulls down imaginations and brings into captivity every thought to the obedience of Christ. It is impossible to worship the Lord and remain discouraged.

Worship represents the voice of the Lord in our midst. In the Book of Hebrews these words are ascribed to Jesus: "I will declare thy name unto my brethren, in the midst of the church will I sing praise unto thee" (Heb. 2:12). In an actual worship service where the body of Christ shares in prophecy, spiritual songs, and exhortation, who is speaking? Paul tells us here that it is Jesus speaking. Each believer is contributing, bringing to one another the full message of Christ. If we fail to receive from our brothers and sisters in a corporate expression of worship, we will miss much of what God is speaking to the Church.

Worship enables us to rightly divide the Word of truth. The Old Testament pattern of God's provision for His people to receive the Word serves as an example for the Church today. The prophet Ezekiel described the order of the priestly ministry, which is a perfect prototype of God's purpose for His ministry today:

> But the priests the Levites…they shall come near to me to minister unto me…. And they shall teach my people the difference between the holy and profane, and cause them to discern between the unclean and the clean.
>
> —Ezekiel 44:15, 23

The order of worship established here is first faithfulness, then worship, then teaching. In faithfulness these Old Testament ministers were to draw near to the Lord. So we must have a daily communion and fellowship with Him, becoming intimately acquainted with the Lord. Then they were to worship: "They shall come near to me to minister unto me." Finally, they were to teach the people and cause them to discern between good and evil. So who is qualified to minister and rightly divide the Word of truth? Is it the one who draws from natural ability and good training, or the one who has been in the presence of the Lord? It is in the presence of the Lord that we receive revelation of the Word. Since that is true, should we not make certain that our contact with God is fresh and living in order that the spirit of wisdom and revelation in the knowledge of Him is our portion (Eph. 1:17)? As we are obedient to God, we become enraptured with the Person of the Lord Jesus Christ. Our needs become secondary, and pleasing the Father takes precedence in our lives over everything else.

Praise and worship, both private and corporate, need to become priorities with the people of God. We should cry with the psalmist, "I will bless the Lord at all times: his praise shall continually be in my mouth" (Ps. 34:1). Only then can we expect to enjoy the benefits God intended for His people. As we focus on the goodness of God, our hearts will be filled with gratitude and our automatic response will be to praise Him.

Communion

We have studied communion in a broad sense as the expression of prayer that applies to all of communication between God and man. The eternal plan of God, which included sending the Third Person of the Holy Spirit to the earth, is ultimately realized when that relationship of communion is established in the hearts of men and women who accept salvation through the blood of Christ. In its purest essence, however, true communion with God is the result of a deeply personal love relationship with Him. Jesus said, "Behold, I stand at the door, and knock: if any man hear my voice, and open the door, I will come in to him, and will sup with him, and he with me" (Rev. 3:20). As we come into the place of worship in the presence of God and experience the joy of relationship with Him, we can commune with Him in a very intimate way. He desires to have this personal fellowship with us so He can speak quietly to our spirits and we can hear His voice of love speaking to us.

Intimacy in relationship involves two persons who want to share their love with each other. God, who is love, desires to share that love personally to every heart that will invite the Holy Spirit to reveal Jesus to it. God wants to share His love with us in a way that impregnates us with the living Word. As He lifes us by His Spirit, we can take that divine life to others by sharing His living Word. As we learn to give our love to Him in worship, we begin to know His loving response to us in the intimacy of communion. Paul prayed for the Corinthians, "The grace of the Lord Jesus Christ, and the love of God, and the communion of the Holy Ghost, be with you all. Amen" (2 Cor. 13:14). Through this intimate relationship of communion with God we experience the reality of His love and Person in such a way that He can never again be just a creed or an influence in our thinking. He becomes a Person to be loved and obeyed, a Person who is more real than any other on earth.

God's purpose for creating mankind was to commune with him and share His love with him. Redemption involves the entire Godhead working together to bring man back into that love relationship. Our initial salvation experience does not complete the work of redemption; it only starts that process. As we cultivate a life of prayer, we continually come into a more intimate relationship with God that satisfies not only our hearts, but His as well.

Summary

Learning to commune with the Holy Spirit makes us more sensitive to His other moods. We then learn to know Him as a Person and can cooperate with His purposes as He executes them through His offices and expresses them through His moods. The Holy Spirit can then anoint our eyes to see and our ears to hear the will of God for every moment of our lives. At last our hearts will be satisfied as we, in turn, satisfy the heart of the Father in this most intimate of prayer relationships: communion with God.

The Holy Spirit is clearly revealed as a divine Person throughout the Scriptures. We can know this wonderful Third Person of the Godhead in all the beautiful facets of His personality as we seek Him in prayer and in the Word.

In the second and third books in this series about the Holy Spirit we will learn more explicitly how to enter into a personal relationship with Him and walk in the Holy Spirit's anointing through the baptism of the Holy Spirit. We will also study the purposes of the gifts and fruit He brought to the Church and learn how to be led by Him as children of God. Paul taught, "For all who are being led by the Spirit of God, these are sons of God" (Rom. 8:14, NAS).

We can safely conclude, then, that we must learn to be led by the Spirit of God to come to maturity and be called sons of God. In *Walking in the Anointing of the Holy Spirit*, we will learn that adoption as sons of God happens at maturity and signifies that we are true sons of God with knowledge. As we come to maturity, we can defeat the enemies pursuing us. The Spirit of God leads us into personal victory and teaches us how to win in spiritual warfare, pulling down strongholds that would try to defeat us. He will enable us to be a part of His living organism, the Church that He is building in the earth. And He will teach us how to receive our inheritance in Christ. It is our responsibility to cultivate this divine relationship so we can "reign in life through the One, Jesus Christ" (Rom. 5:17, NAS).

Notes

Chapter 1
Relationship With a Divine Personality

1. Fuchsia Pickett, *God's Dream*, (Shippensburg, PA: Destiny Image, 1991).

Chapter 2
Emotional Responses of the Holy Spirit

1. Scripture references to God's emotions include: Genesis 6:3, 6; Genesis 18:32; Leviticus 26:28; Joshua 7:26; Psalm 78:65; Isaiah 1:24; Jeremiah 7:13; Hebrews 10:12.

2. John Rea, *The Holy Spirit in the Bible* (Lake Mary, FL: Charisma House, 1990), 128.

Chapter 3
Emblems Reveal the Holy Spirit's Character

1. Ada R. Habershon, *The Study of the Types* (Grand Rapids, MI: Kregel Publications, 1980), 11–13.
2. Rea, *The Holy Spirit in the Bible*, 21.
3. Ibid., 274.
4. Ibid.

Chapter 4
The Sevenfold Power of the Holy Spirit

1. E. Y. Mullins, *International Standard Bible Encyclopedia*, Vol. 3, James Orr, ed. (Grand Rapids, MI: Wm. B. Eerdman's, 1976), 1406–1417.
2. Ibid.

CHAPTER 5
SEVEN MOODS OF THE HOLY SPIRIT, PART I

1. Noah Webster, *American Dictionary of the English Language*, 1828.

Uncover the Ultimate Purpose in Your Life

Dr. Fuchsia Pickett is a highly respected and deeply loved woman of God who has been referred to as one of the "best Bible teachers of our times," and now you know why!

We pray that *Understanding the Personality of the Holy Spirit* has helped strengthen your daily walk. Here are two more awesome opportunities to sit under her anointed teaching and draw closer to God.

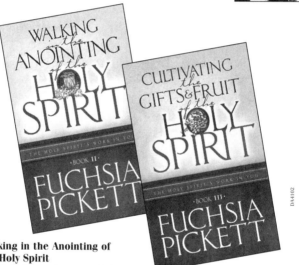

Walking in the Anointing of the Holy Spirit
Dr. Pickett introduces you to her best Friend and Teacher as He revealed Himself through the Scriptures to her personally.
1-59185-284-6 $12.99

Cultivating the Gifts and Fruit of the Holy Spirit
Develop an intimate relationship with Christ, learn to abide in Him, and become a fruitful Christian.
1-59185-285-4 $12.99

Step into *His* will and *your* full potential!

Charisma®
HOUSE
A STRANG COMPANY
Everything good starts here!
3505c

Call 800-599-5750
Visit your local Christian bookstore
Or order online at charismahouse.com